Andros Island Travel and Tourism

Travel Guide and Locations information

Author
Michael Thomson

Copyright Notice

Copyright © 2017 Global Print Digital
All Rights Reserved

<u>Digital Management Copyright Notice</u>. This Title is not in public domain, it is copyrighted to the original author, and being published by **Global Print Digital**. No other means of reproducing this title is accepted, and none of its content is editable, neither right to commercialize it is accepted, except with the consent of the author or authorized distributor. You must purchase this Title from a vendor who's right is given to sell it, other sources of purchase are not accepted, and accountable for an action against. We are happy that you understood, and being guided by these terms as you proceed. Thank you

First Printing: 2017.

ISBN: 978-1-912483-37-2

Publisher: Global Print Digital.
Arlington Row, Bibury, Cirencester GL7 5ND
Gloucester
United Kingdom.
Website: www.homeworkoffer.com
.

Table of Content

Introduction 1
History 4
The People, Culture and Lifestyle............................24
  Ethnicity, Language, & Religion............................. 27
  Social Life.. 32
Travel and Tourism..36
  Attraction 52
    Beaches...56
  Activities 59
    Diving... 67
    Fishing.. 72
    Snorkeling.. 76
  Tradition On Andros Island..................................... 82
  Archeological Museum... 84
  In Depth 86
  General Information 90
  Andros Travel Information 95
  Planning a Trip 99
  Accommodations.. 108
    All Inclusive 116
    Eco Tourism 121
    Hotels.. 127
    Villa Rentals 133
  Transportation 137
    Air Travel 143
    Ferries... 147
    Rental Cars... 150
    Sailing & Boating.. 156
    Taxis 159
  Restaurants 163
  Weather 165

Introduction

The largest island in The Bahamas, Andros is an excellent budget destination. One of the Western Hemisphere's biggest unexplored tracts of land is still quite mysterious. Mostly flat, its 5,957 sq. km (2,300 sq. miles) are riddled with lakes and creeks, and most of the local residents who still indulge in fire dances and go on wild boar hunts on occasion live along the shore.

Andros is 161km (100 miles) long and 64km (40 miles) wide. Its interior consists of a dense tropical forest, truly rugged bush, and many mangroves. The marshy and relatively uninhabited west coast is called "the

Mud," and the east coast is paralleled for 193km (120 miles) by the world's third-largest underwater barrier reef, which drops more than 167km (104 miles) into the Tongue of the Ocean, or TOTO. On the eastern shore, this "tongue" is 229km (142 miles) long and 1,000 fathoms (1.8km/1 mile) deep.

Lying 274km (170 miles) southeast of Miami and 48km (30 miles) west of Nassau, Andros actually comprises three major land areas: North Andros, Central Andros, and South Andros. In spite of its size, Andros is very thinly populated (its residents number only around 5,000), although the tourist population swells it a bit. The temperature range here averages from 72° to 84°F (22°-29°C).

You won't find the western side of Andros written about much in yachting guides tricky shoals render it almost unapproachable by boat. The east coast, however, offers kilometers of unspoiled beaches and is studded with little villages. Lodgings that range from simple guest cottages to dive resorts to fishing camps have been built here. "Creeks" (we'd call them rivers) intersect the island at its midpoint. Also called "bights," they range in length from 8 to 40km (5-25 miles) and are dotted with tiny cays and islets.

The fishing potential at Andros is famous, spawning records for blue marlin catches. Divers and snorkelers find that the coral reefs here are among the earth's most beautiful, and everyone loves the pristine beaches

History

One of the first inhabitants of Andros were the Phoenicians. According to some historians, the capital of Andros was the Phoenician town of Arados which later became Andros. Then came the Cretans whose leader was General Andros. One of the most important civilizations of the island was developed in Zagora area which reached its peak between 900-700 B.C. During the Archaic, Classical and Hellenistic periods (600 B.C. - 199 A.D.) Paleopolis (literally meaning the old city) was the capital of the island. Andros contributed to this period with its spiritual and material wealth and especially its naval strength. During the Roman period, the island saw a decline with a small rise again during the years of the Empress Adrianos.

During the years of the first Byzantine Emperor Constantinos, Andros was part of the Empire. The basis for the prosperity in the area was the silkworm trade which occupied most of the inhabitants who used the top floors of their houses to cultivate the silkworms and to produce fine silk materials which were in demand in the capitals of Greece and in Europe and European businessmen came to the island to make their transactions.

After the fall of the Byzantine Empire by the Crusadors in 1204, the Aegean was taken over by the Venetians. The island remained under the Venetian rule until 1566 when it was seized by the Turks. The Venetians, in order to protect the island from the pirates and the Turks, had built castles, towers and lookout posts.

The Turks seize Andros in 1566 but due to privileges which were in force from the beginning of the occupation, the island remained self-governing. Greek schools in Andros started in the 18th century due to an attempt by the Ottoman regime to be more liberal. In the churches and monasteries the priests and monks taught the Greek language together with the values of western enlightenment and along with this came the spiritual re-birth in the shape of Theophilos Kairis who raised the flag for the National Revolution on the tower of the church of St. George in Andros, on March 10th 1821.

During the second half of the 19th century a new bourgeois class emerged made up from the families of those involved in the wealthy shipping business. Ship captains built themselves up into ship-owners and their ships (mostly with names starting with Andros) made the name of Andros famous all over the world. In the past 20 years, along with the shipping business and the rudimentary farming business came the development of the tourist industry with all its positive and negative aspects and which has peaked in the last ten years.

Acient Times

The island owes its name to its first settler, one of the generals of the Cretan king Rodamanthys, called Andros, who was given the island by his sovereign. Being the son of Anios and grandson of Apollo, Andros was of divine descent and his votive offering can still be found at the Oracle of Delphi. In earlier times, the island had various other names: Nonagria, Hydrousa, Lassia and Epagria, all descriptive of the physical appearance of the island, which in those days was covered by dense forests, with a network of brooks and streams.

The island kept its name until the 13th century, when it was re-named by the conquering Franks, who called it the Island of Saint Andreas after its patron saint, whose name however has not been found in any of the island's historical records. Originally, Andros was settled by subsequent waves of different peoples: Kareans, Phoenicians, Minoan Cretans, Argeians, Egyptians, and finally Ionians who settled here before the arrival of the Dorians.

Thanks to its fertile soil the island flourished, and during the second Hellenic colonisation in the 8th century B.C. its inhabitants founded many colonies along the coastline of the Chalkidiki peninsula and Thrace, including Stagera, the birth place of Aristotle. Zagora, an important settlement of the Geometric era (9th - 7th century B.C.), bears witness to the remarkable cultural flourishing of this region. The island continued to thrive throughout the 6th century B.C. when it constituted an independent state with its own coins.

During the Persian wars Andros was occupied for ten years by the Persians, and following their defeat at Salamina, it became part of the Athenian Alliance until the first Pelopponesian War, at the end of which it changed sides and became an ally of Sparta. Today's old part of Andros Town (Palaeopolis) on the west coast was then already the centre of the island and remained so until the 4th century B.C.

In the Macedonian and Hellenistic wars Andros shared the fate of the rest of the Cyclades, but in 199 B.C. it was occupied by the Romans who drove the inhabitants out of the island and as far as Delios in Boiotia. The Romans were initially interested only in the spills of war, but they eventually took possession of the island in the 1st century B.C. when it became part of the Provinces of the Islands.

Middle ages

From the beginning of the Byzantine era Andros distinguished itself as a seat of learning and the neoplatonic philosopher Proklos (412-485) taught there for many years. In the 9th century, presbyter Michael Psellos founded an Academy of Philosophy on the island, where many Athenians were educated, including the philosopher Leon, who became a great astronomer and geometrist of his time.

In the 11th and 12th century the island experienced an economic boom, becoming the centre of silk-weaving industry and exporting exquisite velvet fabrics known as examita or zentata, which were highly valued in the West and were sent as gifts to the German imperial court. At the same time, during the entire Middle Ages, the island suffered raids from pirates and Saracens. Following the fall of the Byzantine Empire to the Franks in 1204, Andros was dominated by the Venetians and ruled by Governor Marino Dandolo, followed by Governor Sanoudo and later by various descendants of aristocratic families. At that time, many towers and forts were erected on the island, and some partially survive until today.

In 1416 and 1468 Andros was attacked by the Turkish fleet and looted. In 1537 it was taken over by Chaoreddin Barbarossa and subjected to Turkish taxes, eventually becoming part of the Ottoman Empire in 1579.

Modern times

Under the Ottoman rule the island was part of the Cyclades sanjak (province) ruled by kaptan pasha (admiral of the fleet). Later it was bestowed on the sultan's mother, Sultana Velide, and in 1774 on the sister of the future Sultan Selim. At that time Andros had many privileges, as it was no longer directly dependent on kaptan pasha and was ruled by various kodjabashis (local lords). Turkish rule was temporarily interrupted by the Russian occupation of the Cyclades in 1770-1774.

On the 10th of May 1821, the renowned cleric and teacher of the nation Theophilos Kaoris declared a revolution on Andros, and the island contributed to the anti-Turkish revolutionary effort with substantial numbers of men and quantities of provisions, as described in the historical records of the period. Two schools were active on the island during the Ottoman rule: the School of Greek in Kato Kastro (Chora) and the School of Agia Triada in Korthi.

Andros island was very important in ancient times, thanks to its wealth, both material and intellectual, but most af all thanks to its naval power.

A few stone and bronze age findings testify the existence of prehistoric settlements in the island. Our knowledge comes from mythology. The founder and first king of the island was Andros. The island was later colonized by Pelasgians.

Ancient times

During historic times the island was inhabited by Ionians, who possibly came from Athens, as Thoukydidis records. Latin Plinius the senior preserved some of the names, the poets were calling the island. According to Myrtilos it was called Gavros and later Antandros. Kallimachos calls it Lasia, others Hydrousa and others Nonagriam and Epagrim (the last two meaningless words in greek). These names represent physical characteristics of the island, vegetation, water, etc.

Significant information about Andros during Geometric Time, comes from the discovery of an important settlement, rare for the time period, in the area of Zagora. The settlement flourished during 700-500 B.C. and, as it seems, vanished abruptly.

In Zagora were found 45 rectangular rooms with storage areas and yards, built with the andriotic all-time stone material, schist. Floors were covered with a layer of compressed mortar, as was common technique till recently. The layers of mortar at the roof were supported by wooden beams and schist plates.

An important building of the settlement was the later-built temple, which was probably dedicated for the worship of Goddess Athena.

During 7th century B.C. Andros was the metropolis of four important colonies in the areas of Chalkidiki and Strymon bay, in northern Greece. These were Akanthos, Sani,Stagiros and Argilos. According to Herodotus, during Persian Wars the Andriots, as well as the other islanders, seem to have been with the Persian side, offering "soil and water" to them.

The center during Classical Times, main city and information center to us, is the settlement, which was built at the present town of Paleopolis. The town seems to have been established around 700 B.C., when Zagora was abandoned. No systematic excavations have been made yet. Two findings by chance are very important, Hermes of Andros (Hellenistic copy) and the hymn to Goddess Isis, the latter still being used as a door lintel in a house in Paleopolis.

There was also an acropolis, port, agora (market) and sufficient fortification. About 60 silver and bronze coins have been found, many of which portray Dionysos, loved God in Andros.

During Peloponnesian War Andros lined up with its allies, Athenians, offering ships and soldiers. As a member of the Athenian Alliance, Andros was paying 72000 drachmas (12 talanta), as an island tax to the alliance fund.

In 411 B.C. Andriots broke away from Athens, lined up with Sparta, but came back and participated in the 2nd Athenian Alliance in 378 B.C.

After the battle in Haeronia in 338 B.C., where they fought allied with Athenians, the city-state of Andros came under Macedonian rule.

During Hellenistic historic period, which follows the death of Alexander the Great, Andros was under direct Macedonian control and participated in the islands community. Between 315 B.C. and 31 B.C., was consecutively under roman, macedonian, ptolemean and second macedonian, under Dimitrios, rule. In 199 B.C. roman and pergamean troops landed, sieged and captured Paleopolis. Andros was under Pergamos of Attalides till was given to the Romans. Important monument of hellenistic times is the Agios Petros Tower

Byzantine era

In early Byzantine period Andros was an administrative part of Islands Prefecture (capital Rodos). Christianity was spread from the first centuries to its inhabitants.

The geographical position on the main sea route towards Constantinople and the protection needs of the empire from arab pirate attacks, made Andros an important administration center of the Aegean Sea Province (Thema) and base of empire customs. Accordingly was the economic and intellectual prosperity of this period.

We know that about 820 A.C. Leon the Mathematician was instructed rhetoric, philosophy and mathematics in Andros, studing at the same time the rich monastery libraries of the island.

12th century, period of Komninon reign, is the best documented for the island. Valuable sourses of information are the foreign travellers who stopped there, on their trip to Holy Lands.

Anglosaxon Seawurf, who passed from Andros in 1204, informs us that silk industry was the main occupation of the inhabitants. Most prized were mainly the andriotic sixtimes-woven silk textiles. heavy and luxurious, and the fine-wooven "zentata" and "skindalia", fine golden threads.

Despite of the general prosperity we know that enemy raids continued.Venetians, Normands and Genoats repeatedly attacked and ravaged the place.

After the fall of Constantinople by the crusaders, Andros came in Venetian hands. In 1207 it was given to Marino Dandolo, relative of the Doge of Venice and stayed under their rule till 1566. In order to protect the island from consecutive pirate attacks and the Turks, Venetians built defensive castles and towers.

First and main fort of Dandolo, military and administrative center of the Venetian conqueror, was Mesa Kastro (Inner Castle), which was the first core of the later Kato Kastro-Castel a basso (Lower Castle), the middle-age settlement of present day Chora. Present name Riva comes from Venetian times, since in that area was the main dock of Chora.

Verified byzantine churches in Andros are:

Taxiarchis in Messaria (1158)
Taxiarchis in Melida (11th century)
Taxiarchis in Ipsilou (11th century)
Panagia (Virgin Mary) in Mesathuri (12th century)
Agios Nikolaos in Korthi (12th century)

Byzantine fortifications probably existed in present day Kastro Faneromenis (Faneromeni Castle) above Kochylou, whereas tower ruins exist up in Melida village, as well as in the base of the small church of Agia Sofia in Pachykavos in Ormos.

The second byzantine fortification, which is considered bigger and stronger, was Epano Kastro-Castel del alto

(Upper Castle). Some coincide Epano Kastro with present day Kastro Faneromenis, while others place it in Paleokastro area, above Ormos. In 19th century were still visible in the area ruins of fortifications, houses, churches, cisterns and wells.

Smaller castles and fortifications were spread all over the island. Their ruins are visible up to date. Some of them are the Pirgos Makrotantalou (Makrotantalo Tower), Briokastro in Varidi, Kastellaki in Gides.

During the Venetian rule also took place the settlement of Albanians, who mainly settled in the northern part of Andros.

Venetian catalogue of 1470 reports that Andros is inhabited by 2000 people, while ottoman report of 1567 mentions 1800 roman-greek and albanian houses and 50-60 Frank houses.

Ottoman occupation

Ottoman occupation of Andros took place in 1566, in accordance with the opinion of the inhabitants. This fact, of the willing subordination, gave the island special privileges. The real administration till 17th century was exercised by descendants of byzantine, frank and andriot families, who had adopted the feudalistic venetian system.

Andros had a favourable treatment by the Ottomans even later. From 18th century belonged as "malikanes", a sort of feud, to Vadile Sultana and in 1778 to Selim's the 3rd sister, Sach Sultana.

Andriots payed predetermined taxes and were excluded from forced work and other payments, were protected from possible ottoman interventions, had secured free trade and their rights of succession.

Between 1770 and 1777 Andros, as well as the rest of Cyklades, was controlled by the Russians, through a local ruler called kantzillieris. After the withdrawal of the Russians it was introduced in Andros the institution of "kotzambasi". Kotzambasis in Kato Kastro (Lower Castle) and Korthi were rich elder landowners. Most of the times were elected for one year and were the real governors in Andros.

The economy of the island continued to be agricultural, but in Kato Kastro had evolved a new class of sailors called "gemitzides", who in 19th century raised their own claims. In 1813 Andros had 40 ships with a tonnage of 2800 tons and about 400 sailors.

In the first years of the Ottoman occupation, the operation of a school is reported, founded in 17th century by Capuchin monks. In 1768 the Archbishop of Andros, Dionysios Kairis, created the "School of Greek Literature". In 1814 was established in Korthi the school of Agia Triada.

Recent History

In May 1821 after a people assembly, the participation of Andriots in the Greek War for Independance was decided, with contribution of soldiers, money and battle ships. From 1822 till 1828 social movements broke out in the island, like the one led by Dimitrios Balis, with main reason the unbearable taxes imposed by the local rulers.

At the same time the island suffered from landings of undisciplined troops called "liapides", who terrorised mainly the villagers.

In Ottoman times the rapid growth of shipping in Andros is observed, which after 1880 transformed from sail to steam powered, according to the new demands. Andriot shipping managed to overcome the crisis of both World Wars and constitutes up todate a main source of wealth for the island.

Michael Thomson

The People, Culture and Lifestyle

The people of Bosnia & Herzegovina are quite diverse in numerous ways, most notably in terms of religion, identity, and culture. Despite the many differences, the differences in the daily way of life in the country is more heavily dependent on location as there are vast differences in the urban and rural lifestyles as well as on employment. Religion also plays a significant role, but few people in the country today are overtly religious.

Nearly half the population is urbanized and the other half lives in more rural areas. For the people in the more rural areas life is often times dependent on farming and agriculture, which is a sector that employees about 20% of the working population. For these people, no matter their religion, life is based off the land as days run from sun up to sun down and their wellbeing is heavily dependent on the weather and seasons.

Much of the urban population has more steady jobs in terms of hours and pay, but there are few guarantees in employment in Bosnia & Herzegovina as nearly half the population is unemployed today. For those lucky enough to have a steady job most work somewhat regular hours, generally from about 8:00 am to 4:00 pm. Schools also tend to have regular hours so greatly contribute to the daily way of life.

However, due to high levels of unemployment and strong family and community ties, most of the people that do work tend to share their income with other family members who are struggle to find work. In this way entertainment and spending money on non-essentials is uncommon, but does exist, particularly in the cities. Since there is little money to be spent on recreation and, more importantly, because of such strong family ties, free time, on both evenings and weekends (Saturday-Sunday) is generally spent with family.

Identity

In Bosnia & Herzegovina, the people primarily identify by their religion, the Croatians are Catholic, the Serbs are Orthodox, and the Bosniaks are Muslim. This identity is so powerful, each group is willing to kill and die for it, despite the declining participation in religious ceremonies by each group. Today cities remain divided between Catholic and Muslim, Muslim and Orthodox, Orthodox, and Catholic and none are willing to cross that line in fear of physical harm. Oddly, the people are very similar, if not identically on both an ethnic and linguistic level, but again claim these ethnicities and languages to be distinct from each other. Despite all the similarities, religion trumps all else, but due to different religions, varying foods and cultural aspects have arisen, giving each of these three groups a number of distinctions, which expand beyond just religion.

Ethnicity, Language, & Religion

Ethnicity

The Bosniaks (Muslin citizens of Bosnia & Herzegovina) are the largest ethnic group in the country, however they don't make up a majority. The Serbs and the Croats also make up large percentages of the population, making the country very "ethnically" diverse. These three groups are nearly identical on a genetic level so some would argue there is only one ethnicity in the country. None-the-less, each group claims to be a different ethnicity, a claim magnified by religious, cultural, and political differences. Despite the debate on the ethnic differences between the groups, all agree they are each southern Slavs, very closely related to the Slovenes, Bulgarians, and Macedonians.

Language

The people of Bosnia & Herzegovina all speak the same southern Slavic language (in English commonly called Serbo-Croatian), but the Bosniaks call this language to Bosnian, the Serbs call it Serbian, and the Croats call it Croatian. The most significant difference between the three is that Serbian is generally written in the Cyrillic script, while the other two are written in the Latin script. In Bosnia & Herzegovina only Bosnian and Croatian are official languages.

English is a growing second language, but is a long way from being common in the country. Other popular international languages like French, German, and

Spanish are taught in very small numbers, but all are growing in popularity.

Religion

For the most part, ethnicity is defined by religious affiliation in Bosnia & Herzegovina; the Bosniaks are Muslim, the Serbs are Orthodox, and the Croats are Catholic.

Islam (the name of the religion, whose followers are called Muslims) is a monotheistic religion, whose holy book is called the Qur'an. The Qur'an is believed to be the word of God spoken through the prophet Muhammad from 609-632 CE (Common Era is preferred over AD (Anno Domini or "year of the Lord") since the Islamic world doesn't believe Jesus was the messiah). Islam believes Muhammad was the last prophet sent to earth by God, the last in a long line of prophets, which includes Moses, Abraham, and Jesus among others.

Muslims follow five pillars of their faith: testimony, prayer, alms-giving, fasting, and pilgrimage. These pillars, and other tenants of their faith, can give great structure to their lives as some foods, like pork, are forbidden and every Muslim is expected to pray five times a day. However, the level of participation in each of these pillars and to what degree Islam influences an individual's life varies from person to person and community to community.

Catholicism is a Christian religion that is one of the first Christian religions (founded after the death of Jesus in about 30-33 AD). Catholicism believes that there is a single God who created everything, a savior, the son of God, Jesus Christ who is the forgiver of sins, and there is the Holy Spirit, which makes up the last part of the Holy Trinity. Catholics follow the teachings of the Bible, consisting of the Old and New Testaments. Much of the faith is based on the life and teachings of Jesus, which is found in the gospels (in the New Testament).

Orthodoxy is a Christian religion that claims to be the most loyal to the Christian faith and religion as it was described by Jesus and the Gospels in the New Testament. Christianity, including Orthodoxy, was founded after the death of Jesus in about 30-33 AD; various branches of Orthodoxy were officially recognized by governments long before Catholicism was recognized in the Roman Empire.

Orthodoxy and Catholicism have many of the same beliefs; both believe that there is a single God who created everything and a savior, the son of God, Jesus Christ who is the forgiver of sins. However, Orthodoxy is decentralized so each bishop oversees their local country or region, giving each orthodox country a different leader. In this way, no bishop has more power than any other, meaning the tenants and interpretations of the faith remain relatively unchanged. These beliefs are based on the teachings of the Bible, consisting of the Old and New Testaments, in particular the life and teachings of Jesus, which is found in the gospels (in the New Testament).

Social Life

Behavior

Most of the behavioral rules and restrictions in Bosnia & Herzegovina are based on Islam as a large number of people in the country are Muslim, but more recent cultural history has altered many of these cultural aspects so today how the people of Bosnia & Herzegovina behave is a combination of European and Islamic in origin.

As a visitor to Bosnia & Herzegovina just try to follow the lead of the locals by dressing in alike manner (see below for details), dining in the local etiquette (see our Bosnia & Herzegovina Dining & Food Page), and avoid sensitive conversation topics, such as politics, finances, and business unless initiated by your local counterpart.

Also try to avoid being loud, rude, or showing off wealth.

Dress

The traditional dress in Bosnia & Herzegovina is diverse due to the diversity of the people, the mountainous landscape, and the changes throughout history. Generally, this traditional dress is divided to include the traditional dress of the ethnic Bosniaks, the ethnic Serbs, and the ethnic Croats. However, all three groups of people wore common early European clothing, which included dresses for the women and shirts with pants for the men.

For the Bosniaks, who are Muslims, the dress has characteristics of Turkey, but is more European in style. For the Bosniaks, dresses on women with shirts with pants was the norm, however embroidery was often times absent, which is a change from the Serbs and Croats. Bosniak women also never wore aprons, which was a common piece of clothing with the Serbs and Croats. For the Serbs, most outfits included embroidery in red, with many women wearing loose-fitting long-sleeved shirts, a long apron, embroidered socks, and a belt. Men generally wore similar shirts with knickers.

Both men and women often wore a *jelek*, which is similar to a vest. For the Croat women the dress generally consisted of a white blouse, skirt or tunic, an apron, which was usually quite colorful, sometimes a vest, and a hat or cloth for their hair. For men the dress was generally similar as most men wore dark pants, a colorful belt, a white shirt, and a decorated vest, which was again usually on a dark base to match the pants. Red is a very common color among the Croatians, but this is somewhat regional.

Today, the people of Bosnia & Herzegovina, no matter their ethnicity, tend to wear modern western-styled clothing. The designs and styles of these clothes have little variation from ethnicity to ethnicity, although some more conservative Muslim Bosniaks will always cover their legs, arms, and hair (although this is a rarity in the country).

As a visitor to Bosnia & Herzegovina you are welcome to wear just about any clothing. Just try to dress for the occasion, which means long pants and shirts in mosques, churches, and other more formal locations. Wearing obviously foreign clothing in Bosnia & Herzegovina is not a bad thing either; there are some ethnic tensions in the country and in some places being foreign is better than being a member of a different local ethnicity.

Travel and Tourism

Andros the Ideal Destination

A vacation in Andros is a wonderful, unforgettable experience! The Greek Island of Andros has something for everyone, from ancient sites and historical monuments to lush nature paths and golden sandy beaches. Its excellent tourist infrastructure and its exquisite state-of-the-art museums make Andros Greece attractive to visitors from every corner of the world.

The close proximity of Andros to Athens, has established it as one of the best holiday spots for short and long vacations. The island's connection with other islands in the Cyclades, also make it the perfect stop on an island-hopping adventure.

Andros Greece is irresistible to nature aficionados. It is packed with charming walking paths beside streams and waterfalls that wind through villages. Some very rare flora and fauna can be seen on the walking paths, giving visitors the opportunity to "get in touch" with nature. Andros beaches are abundant and beautiful, especially the ones that are located in quaint bays and coves.

The island of Andros Greece has been inhabited since the 10 th century BC, and historical evidence of its importance throughout the ages can be seen in many parts of the island. Ancient cities, century-old towers, impressive monasteries and precious relics displayed in museums for all visitors.

Andros Greece possesses an extremely wide variety of hotels, dining and nightlife venues and other tourist facilities. It is a well-organized island that caters to thousands of tourists every year. There are Andros hotels for all budgets, entertainment venues for all musical tastes and dozens of shops and boutiques that carry everything a visitor of Andros will ever need.

Andros Hotels

On the Greek Island of Andros, visitors will find an inexhaustible array of accommodations that satisfy all preferences and needs. You can be sure that you will be provided with the ideal Andros hotel accommodation that will cater to your personal style and taste. In the Andros Island vacation resorts of Batsi, Gavrio and Andros Town, there are both luxury and discount Andros hotels for all budgets.

Andros Island is a vacation resort for all types of visitors. Some come for the beaches, some for nature walks and other for the cultural venues. Families and large groups of friends will find Andros hotels that offer spacious hotel rooms, studios and apartments. Couples are provided with romantic Andros hotel suites and rooms with a view of the Aegean Sea. Many hotels offer Andros Island vacation packages, which include accommodation, car rentals, excursions and other services. Enquire at your chosen Andros hotel about the extra services it provides.

Andros Beaches

Imagine lying on soft sands, soaking up the warm rays of the sun, next to waves lapping upon the beach. If this seems like a dream, come to Andros. If you are vacationing on the eastern side of the island, you can visit the Andros beaches of Niborio, which can get quite crowded, or the quieter, pristine sandy Andros beaches of Vori and Achla, which you can reach by tour boat from Andros Town. The Andros beaches of Paraporti, Gialia, and Piso Gialia are lovely and perfect for those who just want to relax in the sun.

The beach with the unusual name "to Pidima tis Grias" is one of the finest beaches on Andros Island, with a large, high rock spurting out of the sea. Along the southern coast of Andros Greece there are the popular beaches of Vintzi, Agia Ekaterini and Kantouni, while if you are in the mood for a bit of peace and quiet, we suggest Bouros, Kalamonari and Kremmydes.

For those who are on holiday on the western side of the island , there is a wide range of splendid Andros beaches to choose from. A good map of Andros can show you the way to them, either by car or footpath. In Batsi, you can visit the long, organized beach of Chryssi Ammos, or if you prefer the superb Andros beaches of Agia Marina, Agios Kyprianos and pebbly Stivari. In nearby Gavrio, the port of the island, you will come across some fine Andros beaches, such as the long, sandy Agios Petros and Fellos. Paleopoli is located on a beautiful bay, with a stunning beach, which you can reach on foot. On the northern coast of Andros Island, you can swim at the beaches of Mikri Peza, Zorkos, Vitali and Ateni.

We suggest renting a boat, acquiring an Andros map and exploring the coast of the island on your own. This way you have access to the remotest and most pristine Andros beaches.

Andros Nightlife – Andros Festivals & Events

In Andros, visitors will find a wide range of entertainment and dining venues. The majority of the Andros nightlife is located in the popular tourist resorts of Batsi, Gavrio and Andros Town. All three have many restaurants and tavernas, as well as bars and clubs to choose from.

For those looking for quieter Andros nightlife, Paleopoli is their best bet. Most Andros Islalnd villages offer quaint tavernas and ouzeries. We suggest having a meal in Apikia and Ormos Korthiou. To get a real "taste" of Andros, you should sample the local cuisine, which is scrumptious. Popular dishes include the island's specialty "froutalia" (omelet with sausage and potatoes), spicy cheese dip, sausages, fried zucchini blossoms, potato-balls, xerotyri (a locally-produced cheese), and a glass of famous Andros wine. Top your meal off with almond sweets, preseves, or kaltsounia (pastries with sweet cheese).

On Andros Island, Greece, visitors can experience the irresistible charm of the island's tradition. A number of festivals and fairs are held throughout the year. In Andros Town (Chora), August 15 is celebrated with a big fair that includes music, dancing and feasting, while during the summer months, Andros Town also hosts several cultural events. Gavrio is the location for the "Gavriotika" festival cultural performances, while in Batsi visitors can take part in the festival of the Monastery of Zoodochou Pigis on July 27. Ormos Korthiou is the location of two of the most important celebrations in Andros Greece: the "Korthiana" fair and the festival of Agios Fanourios on August 27.

We recommend vacationing in Andros, Greece when the wonderful temporary art exhibitions at the Goulandris Museum of Modern Art and the "Ploes" musical events organized by the Petros and Marika Kydonieos Foundation are held.

Andros Sights & Attractions

In Andros Greece, visitors have the opportunity to see a wide variety of sights and attractions. We recommend purchasing a good map of Andros that shows the historical and natural sites throughout the island.

Starting off in the capital of the island, Andros Town (otherwise known as Chora), you should definitely visit the marvellous museums. The Archaeological Museum, which was founded by the Vasilis & Eliza Goulandris Foundation has some very fine exhibits, including most of the ancient artefacts found at the islands archaeological sites. The Maritime Museum in Andros Town displays a wide array of nautical objects, diaries, lithographs and models. The jewel of Andros Town is the Museum of Modern Art, which is also funded by the Goulandris Foundation.

Visitors have the unique chance to see works of some of the finest painters and sculptors from Greece and abroad, including Fassianos, Tsarouchis, as well as frequent displays of works by Picasso, Matisse, Kandinsky, Chagall, and others. The Kairis Library possesses some 3000 rare manuscripts and books, historical archives and art work of the theologian Theofilos Kairis. Other sightseeing in Andros Town includes the Tourlitis Lighthouse, located on a large rock in the middle of the sea, and the Churches of Panagia Theoskepasti and Panagia Thalassini.

For the archaeology enthusiasts, Andros offers several wonderful ancient sites. In Paleopoli, there are two of the finest sites on the island: the Ancient City of Andros and the Geometric Settlement of Zagora, where visitors can see the remains of various structures, including houses, walls, and gates. Paleopoli also has an archaeological museum which displays various aretfacts found at the sites. The Tower of Agios Petros in Gavrio, is one of the best-preserved ancient towers in Greece. Its indoor area contains a spiral staircase that connects 5 levels. Ancient Ispili is located on a hill near the town of Batsi, and includes a number of structures. Excavation of Ispili is ongoing.

Elsewhere on Andros Island Greece, you can visit the many impressive churches and monasteries. Probably the most well-known is the Monastery of Zoodochou Pigis in Batsi, while it is also worthwhile visiting the Monastery of Panachrandou, which offers a stunning view of Andros Town and the 12 th century Monastery of Sotiros, near Vitali. The Epano Kastro, located in the Ormos Korthiou site has remains of a Medieval Town.

Andros is a paradise for nature and outdoor sports lovers. The island is scattered with springs and streams, which attract a lot of tourists to Andros. There are several lovely foot paths that are the same as those that existed in ancient times. All you have to do is to secure a reliable map of Andros Greece and make your walking tour a reality. The paths lead through villages, across stone bridges and along lush hillsides. You can stop at the springs and sample the waters, which are believed to have healing properties for various conditions, including kidney and stomach problems. The most visited areas are Apikia, with the Sariza Spring and the Ravine of Pithara, and the village of Remata, with the scenic waterfalls and watermill.

Andros Weather Guide – Andros Climate

Andros, Greece has mild weather throughout the year, with a bit more rainfall than other Cyclades Islands, which is the reason for the island's beautiful vegetation. In, general the weather in Andros is sunny and bright, apart from some showers in the winter months.

Winter weather in Andros is similar to the weather of other Cycladic Islands, with temperatures between 8°C and 13°C. Spring is one of the best times to visit Andros Greece. Temperatures rise, ranging from a pleasant 15°C to 22°C. As the summer comes round, the weather in Andros gets quite warm, but still remains enjoyable, with average temperatures between 24°C and 30°C. Autumn time in Andros, Greece continues to be a wonderful season for vacations, as temperatures range in the mid teens and the low 20s.

The Meltemi wind, which blows in July and August, cool down the hottest months, especially on the northeastern side of Andros Island.

Ferries to Andros

Its close proximity to Athens makes Andros Island a fine location for both long and short holidays. There are frequent ferry boats to Andros from Rafina Port, which is located approximately 30 km from the center of Athens. Ferries to Andros Port in Gavrio are especially frequent during the summer, when the island is a major vacation resort.

The ferry from Rafina to Andros Greece takes approximately 2 hours, while a hydrofoil from Rafina Port takes about 1 hour. If you want to ensure yourself a seat on a ferry to Andros Island, you should book in advance, particularly during the high tourist season.

Apart from Rafina Port, ferries from Andros Port connect the island to other Cyclades Islands (Kea,

Kythnos, Mykonos, Naxos, Paros, Syros and Tinos) and several islands in the Northeastern Aegean cluster, including Chios and Lesvos.

If you are arriving in Greece by airplane at the Athens Airport "Eleftherios Venizelos", you can easily reach Rafina Port by bus or taxi, and from there board a ferry to Andros Island Greece.

Natural beauty and a rich cultural heritage dating back in the centuries

The northernmost of the Cyclades Island Group and second in size only to Naxos, Andros beguiles visitors with its natural beauty and vast cultural heritage, the product of a centuries-long history going back to 3000 B.C.

Following along with the other Aegean islands the fate of the mainland, Andros was successively under the Macedonians, the Romans, the Francs and the Turks. Not exhausted in the Cycladic tradition, local architecture includes typical Aegean samples harmoniously co-eisting with neoclassic mansions, tower-houses and stone buildings. Today, one can visit four monasteries of the 14th and 15th century A.D., as well as a plethora of churches dating back at the time of Nikiforos Fokas, such as the Sanctuary of Taxiarches at the Messaria village that is of great historical value.

Andros is blessed with a "waterproof" rocky ground that bestows it with many water-fountains, brooks, waterfalls and rivers with rich vegetation, maple trees and walnut trees growing on their banks. The valley of Dipotamaton is the site of tens of watermills and other water-powered industries in good condition. The valley has been proclaimed a protected area and its structures pre-industrial-era monuments.

Vegetation on the island hosts the typical fauna of the Mediterranean, as well as partridge, falcons and rare predatory birds.

Large sweeps of sandy beaches, easily accessible and with developed tourist infrastructure are located mostly on the western coastline of the island. Visitors seeking peace and wild natural beauty will find it at the beaches located on the northeastern and southeastern coastlines.

In spite of an extended rural road network, a large part of the old cobble-stone alleys and paths connecting the settlements and the villages survives in good condition, nowadays used by nature lovers that want to visit some of the isolated beauties of the island on foot. The events that compose the identity of the island establish Andros as the cultural capital of the Cyclades. The Museum of Contemporary Art organizes on a yearly basis exhibition with artworks of internationally accredited artists. During the summer of 2004, the museum will host the International Art Exhibition with the works of Pablo Picaso. The choir festival in June is an institution; the local cultural associations during the summer months organize traditional feasts with local dances, food and drink. Also, in Andros takes place the International Festival of traditional dances and folklore traditions and the International Festival of Aegean cuisine.

The traditional Andriotic dish is "fourtalia", an omelet made with potatoes and home made sausage accompanied with local cheese and wine. Visitors should not miss the famous sweets ('amygdalota" and "kaltsounia"), the local ecological honey variety and the fruit preserves.

Attraction

Andros is largely unexplored, and for good reason getting around takes some effort. With the exception of the main arteries, the few roads that exist are badly maintained and full of potholes. Sometimes you're a long way between villages. If your car breaks down, all you can do is wait and hope that someone comes along to give you a ride to the next place, where you'll hope to find a skilled mechanic. If you're heading out on your own, make sure you have a full tank of gas service stations are few and far between.

At present, not all of Andros can be explored by car. We hope that as the island develops, roads will be constructed so that it will be easier to get around. Most of the driving and exploring is currently confined to North Andros; even there, roads go only along the eastern sector past Nicholl's Town, Morgan's Bluff, and San Andros.

Bird-watchers are attracted to Andros for its varied avian population. In the dense forests, in trees such as lignum vitae, mahogany, Madeira, horseflesh, and pine, dwell many birds, including parrots, doves, marsh hens, and whistling ducks.

Botanists are lured by the wildflowers of Andros. Some 40 to 50 species of wild orchid are said to thrive here, some of which can be found nowhere else. New discoveries are always being made, as more botanists study the land's rich vegetation.

If you're driving on Central or South Andros, you must stay on the rough Queen's Highway. The road in the south is paved and better than the one in Central Andros, which should be traveled only for emergency purposes or by a local.

On Central Andros, near Small Hope Bay Lodge at Fresh Creek, you can visit the workshop where Androsia Batik (tel. 242/368-2080; www.androsia.com) is made. These are the same textiles sold in the shops of Nassau and other towns. Here, artisans create designs using hot wax on fine cotton and silk fabrics. The fabrics are then crafted into island-style wear, including blouses, skirts, caftans, shirts, and accessories. All are hand-painted and hand-signed, and the resort wear comes in dazzling red, blue, purple, green, and earth tones. You can visit the factory Monday through Friday from 8am to 5pm, Saturday from 9am to 2pm.

Morgan's Bluff, at the tip of North Andros, lures people hoping to strike it rich. The pirate Sir Henry Morgan supposedly buried a vast treasure here, but it has eluded discovery to this day, though many have searched.

Located off the northwestern coast of Andros, Red Bay Village is the type of place that continues to make these islands seem mysterious. In the 1840s, Seminoles and people of African descent escaping slavery in Florida fled to Andros and, miraculously, remained hidden until about 50 years ago, when an explorer "discovered" their descendants, who remain a very small, virtually self-sufficient tribe, living just as the Seminoles did in the Florida Everglades some 2 centuries ago. You should be polite and ask permission before indiscriminately photographing them. Red Bay Village is connected by a causeway to the mainland, and tourists can get here by road from Nicholl's Town and San Andros.

Beaches

Beaches on Andros

There is a lot to recommend a getaway on Andros Island, from the expansive national park system to the fact that it is the Bonefish Capital of the world. One thing remains true about almost every person to visit the island -- they always leave room for at least a few hours on the beach. Surrounding the island is the third largest barrier reef in the world, which means calm surf and smooth sands are a commonplace.

Beach Choices in The Area

There are a large number of beaches to enjoy in the area. Snorkeling is an option at some locations, for those who enjoy this relaxing pastime. For a detailed article concerning any one of these beaches just click on the names of the ones you are intrigued by.

Love Hill Beach: A long stretch of smooth, tan-colored sand, Love Hill Beach leads to Stanyard Creek, an area known for coconut trees.

A second place to consider is Morgan's Bluff Beach. Located at the northern tip of Andros, Morgan's Bluff is a popular spot amongst sailors. In fact, one of the island's top events, the annual All Andros and Berry Island Regatta take place here.

Nicholl's Town Beach: Nicholl's Town Beach is a favorite amongst Nicholl's Town Residents, who enjoy the calm atmosphere and easy swimming.

The beaches on Andros are summarized in the chart below.

BEACHES IN ANDROS

Michael Thomson

Name	Location	Island	Coast
Andros Lighthouse Beach	0.5 mi. East-Northeast of Central Andros Town	North Andros Island	East
Goat Cay Beach	1.8 mi. North of Central Andros Town	North Andros Island	West
Love Hill Beach	2.3 mi. Northwest of Central Andros Town	North Andros Island	East
Morgan's Bluff Beach	2.6 mi. North-Northwest of Central Nicholls Town	North Andros Island	North
Nicholl's Town Beach	0.5 mi. East-Northeast of Central Nicholls Town	North Andros Island	North
North Beach	3.6 mi. Northwest of Central Andros Town	Central Andros	North East
Pleasant Bay Beach	8.9 mi. Southeast of Central South Andros Island	South Andros Island	South East

Small Hope Bay Beach	1.3 mi. East-Southeast of Central Andros Town	North Andros Island	East
Small Hope Beach	2.2 mi. Northwest of Central Andros Town	Central Andros	North East
Sommerset Creek Beach	2.7 mi. Southeast of Central Andros Town	North Andros Island	East

Activities

Despite being the largest island in the Bahamas, Andros may well be the least developed of those that are inhabited. You won't find sprawling resorts here. Instead, it is fishing lodges, guesthouses, and small rental properties that take up space. Visitors headed this way don't expect to encounter a lot of activities, instead they are hoping for a peaceful place to collect their thoughts – and maybe do a little fishing or diving while they are at it.

Diving

Divers coming to Andros will be pleased to know that the Andros Reef is less than a ten minute boat ride from shore. This makes the island a great spot to enjoy, or learn, scuba.

You'll find several dive operators and at least 8 different dive sites in the area. Read Diving page in this book dedicated to diving in this area if you want to discover more specifics.

Beaches & Outdoor Pursuits

Golf and tennis fans should go elsewhere, but if you're seeking some of the best bonefishing and scuba diving in The Bahamas, head to Andros.

Saving Andros for Future Generations The Andros Conservancy and Trust might be called the guardian angel of Andros. This nongovernmental organization was created to preserve and enhance the island's natural assets. In 2002, The Bahamas National Trust began to take on its concerns. Today, nearly 120,000 hectares (296,526 acres) of Andros have been preserved as wetlands, reefs, and marine-replenishment zones doubling the size of the country's national park system.

All this development falls under the general authority of the Central Andros National Park. A great deal of self-policing is involved, with bonefishermen keeping watch over the flats, crabbers protecting local breeding grounds, and divers helping to preserve the reefs. This park is only just emerging, so there are no organized tours, no guides, no nature walks yet. It is still a national park in the making.

Hitting the Beach

The eastern shore of Andros, stretching for some 161km (100 miles), is an almost uninterrupted palm grove opening onto beaches of white or beige sand. Several dozen access points lead to the beach along this shore. The roads are unmarked but clearly visible, and the clear, warm waters offshore are great for snorkeling.

Fishing

Andros is often called the bonefishing capital of the world, and the epicenter of this activity is at Lowe Sound, a tiny one-road hamlet that's 6.5km (4 miles) north of Nicholl's Town. Anglers come here to hire bonefish guides. Cargill Creek is one of the island's best places for bonefishing; nearby, anglers explore the flats in and around the bights of Andros. Some excellent ones, where you can wade in your boots, lie only 68 to 113m (223-371 ft.) offshore.

Whether you're staying in North, Central, or South Andros, someone at your hotel can arrange a fishing expedition with one of the many local guides or charter companies. In particular, Small Hope Bay Lodge, in Andros Town (tel. 242/368-2014), is known for arranging superb fishing expeditions for both guests and nonguests. It also offers fly-, reef, and deep-sea fishing; tackle and bait are provided.

Snokeling & Scuba Diving

Divers from all over the world come to explore the Andros Barrier Reef, which runs parallel to the island's eastern shore. It's one of the world's largest reefs, and unlike Australia's Great Barrier Reef, which is kilometers off the mainland, the barrier reef here is easily accessible, beginning just a few hundred yards offshore.

One side of the reef is a peaceful haven for snorkelers and novice divers. The fish are mostly tame here. A grouper will often eat from your hand, but don't try it with a moray eel. The water on this side is from 2.5 to 4.5m (8 1/4-15 ft.) deep.

On the reef's other side, it's a different story. The water plunges to a depth of 167km (104 miles) into the awesome Tongue of the Ocean (TOTO). One diver claimed that, as adventures go, diving here was tantamount to flying to the moon.

Myriad multicolored forms of marine life thrive on the reef, attracting nature lovers from all over the world. The weirdly shaped coral formations alone are worth the trip. This is a living, breathing garden of the sea, and its caves feel like cathedrals.

For many years, the U.S. Navy has conducted research at a station on TOTO's edge. The Atlantic Undersea Test and Evaluation Center (AUTEC), as the station is called, is devoted to underwater weapons and antisubmarine technologies. It's based at Andros Town and is a joint U.S. and British undertaking.

Among other claims to fame, Andros is known for its blue holes, which drop into the brine. Essentially, these are narrow, circular pits that plunge as far as 60m (197 ft.) straight down through rock and coral into murky, difficult-to-explore depths. Most of them begin below sea level, though others appear unexpectedly and dangerously in the center of the island, usually with warning signs placed around the perimeter. Scattered at various points along the coast, you can get to them either in rented boats or as part of a guided trip. The most celebrated one is Uncle Charlie's Blue Hole, mysterious, fathomless, and publicized by the legendary underwater explorer Jacques Cousteau.

The other blue holes are almost as incredible. Benjamin's Blue Hole is named after George Benjamin, its discoverer. In 1967, he found stalactites and stalagmites 360m (1,181 ft.) below sea level. What was remarkable about this discovery is that stalactites and stalagmites are not created underwater. This has led to much speculation that The Bahamas are actually mountaintops and all that remains of a mysterious continent that has long since sunk beneath the sea (perhaps Atlantis?). Most of the blue holes, like most of the island's surface, remain unexplored. Tour boats leaving from Small Hope Bay Lodge will take you to them.

For good snorkeling, head a few kilometers north of Nicholl's Town, where you'll find a crescent-shaped beach, along with a headland, called Morgan's Bluff, honoring the notorious old pirate. If you're not a diver and can't go out to the Andros Barrier Reef, you can do the second-best thing and snorkel near a series of reefs known as the Three Sisters. Sometimes, if the waters haven't turned suddenly murky, you can see all the way to the sandy bottom. The outcroppings of elkhorn coral are especially dramatic.

Since Mangrove Cay is underdeveloped, rely on the snorkeling advice and gear rentals you'll get from the dive shop at Seascape Inn (tel. 242/369-0342; www.seascapeinn.com). A two-tank dive costs $125 for hotel guests; nonguests are not served.

Small Hope Bay Lodge lies not far from the barrier reef, with its still-unexplored caves and ledges. A staff of trained dive instructors at the lodge caters to both beginners and experienced divers. Snorkeling expeditions can be arranged, as well as scuba outings (visibility underwater exceeds 30m/98 ft. on most days, with water temperatures 72°-84°F/22°-29°C). You can also rent gear here. To stay at the all-inclusive hotel for 7 nights and 8 days (rates include meals, tips, taxes, airport transfers, and three dives per day), you'll pay $2,245 to $2,420 per person, with reduced rates of $1,320 for children. All guests are allowed, at no extra cost, to use the beachside hot tub and the sailboats, windsurfers, and bicycles.

Diving

Scuba Diving Near Andros

The Andros Reef, which is one of the largest barrier reefs in the world, is just a 10 minute boat ride from most docks on Andros. Thanks to preservation efforts by the Andros Conservancy and Trust, the reef remains unspoiled and a beautiful destination for divers of all skill levels. If you're PADI certified, you won't want to skip the chance to view this natural underwater system, and if you aren't certified, don't worry! You can do so through a number of resources while on Andros.

There are several dive operators and at least 8 good dive sites in the area.

Dive Operators

If you'd like to go diving, you should consider Small Hope Bay Lodge Diving. The dive shop at Small Hope Bay Lodge is located right on the dock and can supply guests with all the gear they need for daily dives. The staff is highly-qualified and the equipment is well-maintained. They are located on Andros.

A second option is Tiamo Resorts Diving. Open water dives take guests out to the third largest barrier reef in the world, which is located just about 10 minutes away from the coast by boat. You can call them at (242) 225-6871.

A third option is Andros Diving. Operating out of the Andros Beach Club in Kemp's Bay on South Andros Island is Andros Diving. This operation is known as one of the top dive companies in the area, and has been offering certification courses and open water dives to visitors for over a decade. They're located in southeastern Andros.

Some key facts concerning the area's dive operators are provided right below.

DIVE OPERATORS NEAR ANDROS

Name	Phone	Location	Island
Andros Diving	(954)	9.2 mi. South-Southeast of Central	South Andros

	681-4818	Congo Town	Island
Kamalame Diving	(305) 677-6525	25.2 mi. West-Southwest of Central Clifton Bay	North Andros Island
Small Hope Bay Lodge Diving	(800) 223-6961	2.2 mi. Northwest of Central Andros Town	North Andros Island
Tiamo Resorts Diving	(242) 225-6871	2.7 mi. West-Northwest of Central Congo Town	Central Andros

Dive Services

Check the table below to get a feel for the typical cost of dive services in this area.

DIVE SERVICES		
Offering Type	Low Rate	High Rate
Discover Scuba	$ 100.0	$ 160.0
Double Tank Dive	$ 110.0	$ 240.0

Night Dive	$ 90.0	$ 110.0
Open Water Certification	$ 450.0	$ 850.0
Single Tank Dive	$ 90.0	$ 125.0

Dive Sites

Some information concerning some of the area's dive sites are provided in the table below.

DIVE SITES NEAR ANDROS

Name	Quality	Experience	Max Depth	Latitude	Longitude
Andros Barrier Reef	--	--	--	24.912324643	-77.8967571259
Andros Island - Amphitheatre	Very Good	Advanced Open Water / CMAS **	82.0	24.8650666667	-77.8711
Back Side of the Blue Hole	Good	Open Water / CMAS *	89.9	24.8133833333	-77.84865
Blue Hole 2nd Level	Good	Open Water /	140.1	24.8134666667	-77.8493

		CMAS *			
Blue Hole 3rd Level	Good	--	190.0	24.81285	-77.8490333333
Guardian Inland Blue Hole	Good	--	299.9	24.5113666667	-77.7209833333
Little Frenchman Inland Blue Hole	Good	--	169.9	24.5068666667	-77.72225
Shark Encounter	Excellent	Advanced Open Water / CMAS **	82.0	24.8880666667	-77.5234

To learn more concerning diving, including useful tips and suggestions for both beginners and experienced divers, check out our extensive discussion of diving online in the Caribbean website.

Fishing

Fishing Near Andros

Known as the "Land of the Giants" in the fishing world, Andros is one of the top destinations for bonefishing in the Bahamas. There is even an important bonefish club on the island. If you're interested in spending a day fishing when you visit this island, you'll find a few charter companies ready to help you make it happen.

Fishing while on the Andros Island comes mainly in two forms; the popular fishing charters, and the local tradition of bonefishing.

Bonefishing generally occurs inshore, and so it does not always require a charter. Instead, you will be looking to hire a guide that specialized in fishing in shallow water. Make sure to ask your hotel if they have suggestions, many accommodations have special relations with a particular bonefisher, ensuring you get the best deal.

Andros is famous for this kind of fishing, and in particulr fishing for the elusive bonefish. Catching one takes a bit of skill and a lot of practice. That is why fishermen coming to Andros are always delighted to the bonefish guides and clubs ready to show foreign fishermen the ropes.

If you are considering going fishing during your vacation, you will find two charter fishing operators that can help you find the best fishing spots.

If you'd like to get in contact with a fishing charter, you should consider Bonefish Bradley. Located in the "Bonefish Capital of the World," Bonefish Bradely specializes in reel and fly fishing tours for those who just can't resist getting in a little angling during their island getaway. They are located on Andros Town, Andros.

A second option is Reel Tight Charters. With Reel Right Charters, you can sign up for spear, reef, and deep fishing, as well as kayaking, snorkeling, and scuba diving. You can reach them at (242) 369-2638.

Andros Island Travel and Tourism

The chart directly below summarizes some key facts regarding charters operating in this area.

FISHING CHARTERS IN ANDROS

Name	Type	Phone	Location	Island
Bonefish Bradley	Fishing Charter Service	(305) 677-0475	Andros Town, Northern part of Andros	North Andros Island
Reel Tight Charters	Fishing Charter Service	(242) 369-2638	22.7 mi. East of Central North Andros Island	North Andros Island

You'll find 5 different fishing guides listed below.

FISHING GUIDES IN ANDROS

Name	Type	Phone	Location	Island
Alvin Greene Fishing Guide	Fishing Guide Service	(242) 471-4205	32.9 mi. South of Central Andros Town	Mangrove Cay
Andros Island	Fishing	(242)	Andros Town,	North

Bonefish Club	Guide Service	368-5167	Northern part of Andros	Andros Island
Deneki South Andros Fishing	Fishing Guide Service	(800) 344-3628	1.2 mi. South-Southeast of Central Congo Town	South Andros Island
Mangrove Cay Bonefishing	Fishing Guide Service	(242) 369-0731	9.8 mi. Northwest of Central Congo Town	Central Andros
Philip Rolle's North Andros Fly Fishing	Fishing Guide Service	(242) 329-2661	10.2 mi. Northwest of Central Andros Town	North Andros Island

Snorkeling

Snorkeling Around Andros

The underwater world that surrounds Andros offers snorkelers some of the most diverse and unique sites of all of the Bahamas. Not only does the third largest reef system in the world protect these islands, but it is also home to the highest concentration of blue holes in the world.

Snorkeling is one of the most sought after activities for visitors staying here thanks to these unique features, and many accommodations have begun playing to this by offering not only free gear for guests to use at their leisure, but daily boat trips to some of the top sites as well. If this is not true of your hotel, you can bring your own equipment or rent it from a local dive shop.

In 2002, the government created the Central Andros National Park to promote and sustain the reef, and as a result this area offers some of the healthiest coral in the chain. You can make plans to visit this section and watch as the colorful reef fish dart in and out of the coral, looking for food and sometimes even interacting with visitors. The section of reef off the coast of South Andros is also very well built up and visitors often find themselves in a trance as they sink into the quiet serenity of the calm, clear waters, losing themselves in the movement of the sea creatures that reside here.

As previously mentioned, the amount of blue holes that exist here are is astonishing. These unique natural attractions are freshwater openings in the water that blast fresh water out of the earth several times a day. This is attractive to a variety of marine life and snorkelers can't help but be impressed by the striking blue color of these holes.

Snorkeling Sites

If you're looking forward to exploring below the water's surface you might want to check out Libens Point. A shallow snorkeling site, this destination is known for its elkhorn coral forest and abundance of star coral. This snorkeling site is located on Andros.

Trumpet Reef is another option. With waters that are between three and 15 feet deep, this reef system is great for snorkelers. The sights to be seen include staghorn, brain, and elkhorn coral as well as fish like trumperfish, grunts, angelfish, and yellowtail.

A third location to consider is Andros Barrier Reef. Part of one of the most expansive stretches of barrier reef in the world, this locale is heavily populated by reef fish. This fact makes it a popular stop for both snorkelers and scuba divers, who will be able to spot a number of different species, including snappers, groupers, and parrotfish.

A fourth place where you can go snorkeling is China Point. Known for its remarkably clear waters, even for the area, this site has a nice diversity of marine life. Snorkelers will see brain coral, sergent majors, blue tangs, grouper, trigger fish, squirrelfish, and angelfish regular. If you're interested, this site is found on Andros.

Goat Cay Beach is a fifth location to consider. Popular among beach-goers, this is a small snorkeling site that offers visitors glimpses of schools of reef fish among the sand dollars and sea biscuits

Look through the table below for a quick overview of 9 of the most popular places to enjoy snorkeling in this area.

SNORKELING SITES NEAR ANDROS		
Site	Location	Island
Libens Point	8.1 mi. North-Northwest of Central Andros Town	North Andros Island
Trumpet Reef	2.2 mi. North of Central Andros Town	North Andros Island
Andros Barrier Reef	14.8 mi. North-Northwest of Central Andros Town	North Andros Island
China Point	9.5 mi. Northwest of Central Andros Town	North Andros Island
Goat Cay Beach	1.8 mi. North of Central Andros	North Andros

	Town	Island
Love Hill Beach	2.3 mi. Northwest of Central Andros Town	North Andros Island
North Beach	3.6 mi. Northwest of Central Andros Town	North Andros Island
Red Shoal	11.2 mi. Northwest of Central Andros Town	North Andros Island
Southern Bight Split	3.6 mi. Northwest of Central Congo Town	Central Andros

To learn more concerning snorkeling, including useful tips and suggestions for beginners and "pros" read this detailed discussion of snorkeling in the Caribbean.

The rich sea life and superb conditions in the waters that surround Andros make this destination highly attractive to visitors who often plan strips specifically to take advantage of the snorkeling. Even if this is not your prime goal, you'll still definitely want to make time to put on a snorkel and mask and take a look.

Tradition On Andros Island

The Vassilis and Eliza Goulandri Foundation organizes every summer at the Museum of Modern Arts exhibits of international stature. The Petros and Marika Kydonaeus Foundation organizes modern art and musical fairs mostly known as "Ploes".

The yacht club of Andros founded in 1975 the international open seas sailing of Faliro-Andros-Faliro under the initial organizer, John B. Goulandris. The races are an annual event since their origin, taking place on the last weekend of August every year. The sailing races attract numerous spectators each summer. Occasionally, the antique car races take place which also attract numerous enthusiasts.

The dance festival of the Musical society is given every June. The Development Societies of the island entertain traditionally with Ballo (a local island dance) and Ouzo (the renowned Greek spirit) festivities in the summers.

There are many Andros festivals going on during the summer in Gavrio and the rest of the villages in northwestern Andros:

- ✓ in St Peter on the 29th of June
- ✓ in Makrotandalo on the 17th of July
- ✓ 6th of August
- ✓ 15th of August
- ✓ and the 23rd of August,
- ✓ in Vitali and Gavrio on the 17th of September
- ✓ andin Ammoloho on the 15th of August.

In these festivities, you become part of the Andriot spirit, with food, wine and music from the local folk music players.

The "Gavriotica" is the crowning touch to the summer festivities. The event involves games, folklore exhibition, and folklore feasts at Gavrio Beach with wine, kakavia (a delicious fish soup) and Fourtalia is an omelette made with local sausages.

The Carnival of Gavrion Andros, which takes place the last days of the Carnival festivities, is a traditional feast you should not miss.

Locals will treat you the traditional Andriot Pastries: Amygdalota (almond liqueur crispy cookies), Kaltsounia (walnut and local honey sugar covered pastry), and pasteli

Archeological Museum

The Archaeological Museum is located in the island's capital city Chora. It was founded in 1981, a legacy of the Institution of Vasilis and Eliza Goulandris. It includes preservation's lambs, store rooms, synchronous optical-acoustic systems and security systems.

On the first floor, you can see the copy of Rigas Chartas, informing boards, 3 Mycenaean vases and objects found from the geometrical settlement of Zagora, including photographs and images of the area that show the houses and temple, to give visitors the opportunity to learn all the necessary information about Andros. On the staircase and the ground floor, sculptures and inscriptions of the Archaic, Classical, Roman, Hellenistic, Pre - Byzantine, and Post - Byzantine Times are exhibited. The statue of a naked man known as "Hermes of Andros", a Romaic copy of the 1st century B.C. of the earlier copper statue of

Praxitelis which was found in 1833 in Paleopoli, is very impressive for its size.

Museum of Modern Art
It belongs to the Vasilis and Eliza Goulandris Institution as well. The museum is unique. It is composed of two wards. In the old ward, you can see a permanent exhibition of the creations by M. Tompros, Tsarouchis, Gikas, Moralis, Basiliou, Takis, Fasianos etc.

In the new ward, there is a section of the Institution's collection where exhibitions take place during all the year. The museum also holds exhibitions of painting, sculpture and photography

Naval Museum
An extensive collection of models of ships and several items relevant to the popular naval tradition of the island.

In Depth

In Search of the Chickcharnies

One of the legends of Andros Island is that aborigines live in the interior. These were thought to be a lost tribe of native Arawaks remnants of the archipelago's original inhabitants, who were exterminated by the Spanish centuries ago. However, low-flying planes, looking for evidence of human settlements, have not turned up any indication to support this far-fetched assertion. But who can dispute that *chickcharnies* (red-eyed Bahamian elves with three toes, feathers, and beards) live on the island? Even the demise of Neville Chamberlain's ill-fated sisal plantation was blamed on these mischievous devils. w

The *chickcharnie* once struck terror into the hearts of the superstitious islanders. They were supposed to live in the depths of the Androsian wilderness, making their nests in the tops of two intertwined palm trees. Tales are told of how many a woodsman in the old days endured hardship and misery because he thoughtlessly felled the trees that served as stilts for a *chickcharnie* nest. Like the leprechauns of Ireland, the *chickcharnies* belong solely to Andros. They are the Bahamian version of the elves, goblins, fairies, and duppies of other lands. Children may be threatened with them if they fail to behave, and business or domestic calamity is immediately attributed to their malevolent activities.

The origin of the legend is shrouded in mystery. One story has it that the tales began in the late 19th century when a Nassau hunting enthusiast who wanted to protect his duck-hunting grounds in Andros invented the malicious elves to frighten off unwanted interlopers. Another has it that the myth was brought to The Bahamas by bands of Seminoles fleeing Florida in the early 1880s to escape the depredations of white settlers. Some of the Seminoles settled on the northern tip of Andros. But the most probable explanation is one that traces the *chickcharnie* to a once-living creature an extinct .9m-high (3-ft.) flightless barn owl (*Tyto pollens*) that used to inhabit The Bahamas and West Indies.

According to The Bahamas National Trust, the local conservation authority, such a bird, "screeching, hissing and clacking its bills in characteristic barn owl fashion, hopping onto its victims or pouncing on them from low tree limbs, would have been a memorable sight. And a frightening one."

The species may have survived here into historical times, and Andros, being the largest Bahamian landmass, was probably able to sustain *Tyto pollens* longer than the smaller islands. It is probable that the early settlers on Andros encountered such beasts, and it's possible that *Tyto pollens* was the inspiration for the *Chickcharnie*. In any event, *Chickcharnie* tales are still told in Andros, and there is no doubt that they will live on as a fascinating part of The Bahamas' cultural legacy

General Information

The boat approaches the harbor of Gavrion and you can see the little white houses creating a beautiful sight. Gavrion Andros is peaceful so you will spend your vacation in a relaxing atmosphere.

Gavrio provides you with a wide choice of Andros hotels, rooms, restaurants and entertainment clubs. You will find all kinds of stores in the market as well as local products sold by the producers themselves.

The landscape is characterized by the typical Cycladic beauty; the dovecotes, the wild flowers, the thyme, the sea and the whitewashed chapels each give their own flavor and color to the scenery.

The hamlet of Agios Petros is twenty minutes walk from Gavrion wherein stands the famous round tower dating from Hellenistic Period which is of unknown use for the archaeologists. Some speculate that it might have been an observatory. Take your car and discover the beautiful beaches at the south of Gavrion Andros: Xylokarida, Kipri and Psili Ammos.

Many of them offer the opportunity for water sports. Not far from Gavrion, there is Fellos Beach with its lovely golden beach. As you drive from Gavrion to Batsi an exquisite beauty will unfold before your eyes. The green landscape with the azure sea shimmering under the sun will tempt you to stop, take pictures and jump into the crystal clear sea.

Southern of Gavrion, you will come across Batsi, the most developed and cosmopolitan village in Andros Greece. It has a well organized and sandy beach with shallow waters suitable for small children. There are more beaches for you to see such as Kolona, Stivari, Delevoya and Agia Marina.

If you love water sports, you will not be disappointed. You can hire windsurf boards, canoes, sea bikes, and water-ski.

The remotest Andros beaches (Koutsi beach, Green beach and Paleopolis) can be approached by boat from Batsi or by foot if you love challenges.

The nights in Batsi Andros Greece will be imprinted in your mind for ever. The strolls along the harbor, with the full moon shedding its silver light on your way, the smell of jasmine as you sit at the open-air cinema, the laughter from the bars, the happy faces that walk by will give you something to remember.

To the south of Batsi stands Paleopolis, the old capital of Andros. The sunken old pier can be seen from the road above. The bay attracts many snorkellers and sea lovers. To the North end of Andros, the beaches of Small and Large Peza are waiting for you to enjoy them.

Hora, the capital of Andros Greece, is located on the east coast of the island, built on a peninsula. Hora ends on a little island where the medieval castle is built.

The Venetian castle was used to guard the town against the invading forces. The island is separated from the peninsula of Hora with a narrow sea strip 2-3m and communicates with the land by a stony bridge. AndrosTown (Hora) is divided in two parts; the Old Town and the New. In the Old town, at Riva square, the imposing copper statue of the Unknown Sailor of Andros stands still despite the fierce winds of the Aegean. Saunter in the narrow, picturesque streets of Hora.

There are many shops, cafes and restaurants where you can enjoy local dishes and pastries. The Kydonieos foundation, the archaeological, naval and the two modern art museums hold excellent exhibitions which have rendered Andros Town an important cultural center in Greece.

Nimborio beach, to the left of the town and Paraporti beach to the right will give you the opportunity to enjoy the Aegean sea once more. Near Stenies, the beaches of Yialia and Piso Yialia are worth visiting.

Make an excursion to Sineti, on the green sides of the mountain, northern of Hora. The picture of the stone built houses, dovecotes and watermills in the ravine with the butterflies of the "Panaxia" family, will fascinate you. On the road towards the South East part of the island, the Bay of Korthi with the blue clear waters awaits for you. Enjoy surfing in the beach of Ormos. Visit the beach of St. Catherine, and the remote idyllic creeks of Kalomonari, Boura and St. Giannis in Keramides.

The old Lady's Leap is one of the most famous Androsbeaches. The legend has it that there was an old lady living in the Upper Castle who betrayed the inhabitants to the Turks and after they were slaughtered, she committed suicide by leaping off the rock. The beach is very picturesque with its green waters and the huge rock that

Andros Travel Information

The island of Andros covers 374 sq. km (147 sq. miles). Its highest mountains are the Petalo and the Kouvara (highest peak Prof. Ilias 997 m.). There are four rivers which run across the island from west to east through fertile green valleys ideal for farming. These are the Arni River, which flows into the Bay of Levka, the Big River that flows by the beach at Paraporti (Hora), the Achla River that flows into the Achla Bay and the Double River which runs into the Sineti Bay.

Andros has a great deal to offer. It is the greenest of all the Cycladic islands. The lush vegetation includes oaks, centuries old plane trees, the cypresses, the olive, the walnut and lemon trees. Andros Greece is also famous for its numerous springs. The most famous of all is the "Sariza springs".

Sariza mineral water is best known for properties which aid kidney problems and is bottled in Sariza and distributed all over Greece. Other renowned springs of Andros are Lezina, Zenio at Kouvara, Koumoulos at Menites, Meliti and Metohi at Strapourgies, Abyssos at Levadia and Akoe and Levada at Lamyra. The villages of Andros are ideal for touring. The busiest of them are Andros Town (Hora), the capital of the island, Gavrion, Batsi, Korthio, Apoikia and Paleopolis. Andros beaches are made of fine white sand and small pebbles. Some of them are so remote that they can be accessed only by boat.

You can travel to Andros by ferry boat. You can take the ferry boat from Rafina Port, Attica and arrive at the island within two hours. The boat docks at Gavrion. Ferry boats from Thessaloniki Port depart three times a week for the Cyclades and Crete. If you bring your car along, you will have the chance to tour Andros Island, discover the natural beauty and follow your own schedule. The Meltemia (strong northerly winds of August) are responsible for the cool summers of Andros. Generally, it has a mild climate with temperate winters.

Useful Telephones

> Police Station:

Andros:	+30 22820 22300
Gavrion:	+30 22820 71220
Batsi:	+30 22820 41204
Korthi:	+30 22820 61211
Medical Center:	+30 22820 23703 or 22222

District Medical Office:

Gavrion:	+30 22820 71210
Batsi:	+30 22820 41326

Michael Thomson

Ormos:	+30 22820 61217
Information Center:	
Gavrion:	+30 22820 71770
Hora:	+30 22820 25162
Taxi:	
Hora:	+30 22820 22171
Gavrion:	+30 22820 71171
Batsi:	+30 22820 41081
Kerthi:	+30 22820 62171
Port Police Office:	
Hora:	+30 22820 22250
Gavrion:	+30 22820 71213
Batsi:	+30 22820 41081
Port Police Station:	
Batsi:	+30 22820 41981
Municipality of Andros:	+30 22820 22275

Municipality of Korthi: +30 22820 61219

Municipality of Hydrousa: +30 22820 71250

Planning a Trip

Getting There

By Plane Reaching Andros is not too difficult. Western Air (tel. 242/377-2222 in the U.S.; www.westernairbahamas.com) has twice-daily 15-minute flights from Nassau to the Andros Town Airport, in Central Andros (tel. 242/368-2759). The island is also served by the San Andros Airport in North Andros (tel. 242/329-4000), the Clarence A. Bain Airport on Mangrove Cay (tel. 242/369-0003), and the Congo Town Airport in South Andros (tel. 242/369-2222). Florida Coastal Airlines (tel. 954/772-9808; www.flyfca.net) flies from Fort Lauderdale to South Andros.

Make sure you know where you're going in Andros. For example, if you land at Congo Town on South Andros and you've booked a hotel in Nicholl's Town, you'll find connections nearly impossible at times (involving both ferryboats and a rough haul across a bad highway).

Andros's few available taxis know when the planes from Nassau land and drive out to the airports, hoping to pick up business. Taxis are most often shared, and a typical fare from Andros Town Airport to Small Hope Bay Lodge is about $24.

By Boat Many locals, along with a few adventurous visitors, use mail boats to get to Andros; the trip takes 5 to 7 hours across beautiful waters. North Andros is served by the MV *Lisa J. II,* which departs Potter's Cay Dock in Nassau heading for Morgan's Bluff, Mastic Point, and Nicholl's Town on Wednesday, returning to Nassau on Tuesday. The MV *Captain Moxey* departs Nassau on Monday, calling at Long Bay Cays, Kemp's

Bay, and the Bluff on South Andros; it heads back to Nassau on Wednesday. The MV *Mangrove Cay Express* departs Nassau Wednesday night for a 5 1/2-hour trip to Lisbon Creek, sailing back to Nassau on Monday afternoon. Finally, MV *Lady D*departs Nassau on Wednesday for Fresh Creek, stopping at Staniard Creek, Blanket Sound, and Browne Sound. The trip takes 5 1/2 hours, with the return voyage to Nassau on Sunday. For details about sailing and costs, contact the dock master at Nassau's Potter's Cay Dock at tel. 242/393-1064.

A far more luxurious way to go over the waters is aboard the *Sea Link* or *Sea Wind,* operated by Bahamas Ferries (tel. 242/323-2166; www.bahamasferries.com). The *Sea Link* carries 250 passengers, while the *Sea Wind* seats 180, with another 100 seats available on the open-air deck of each vessel. Trip time varies depending on where you dock on Andros: From Nassau to Fresh Creek, it takes 1 hour and 45 minutes; from Nassau to Driggs Hill, however, it takes 2 1/2 hours.

Island Layout
Chances are, your hotel will be in either Andros Town (Central Andros) or Nicholl's Town (North Andros).

North Andros is the most developed of the major Andros islands. At its northern end, Nicholl's Town is a colorful old settlement with some 600 people and several places that serve local foods. Most visitors come to Nicholl's Town to buy supplies at its shopping complex. North of Nicholl's Town is Morgan's Bluff, namesake of Sir Henry Morgan, a pirate later knighted by the British monarch. Directly to the south of Nicholl's Town is Mastic Point, which was founded in 1781. If you ask around, you'll be shown to a couple of concrete-sided dives that serve up spareribs and Goombay music.

In Central Andros, about 47km (29 miles) south of Nicholl's Town, is Andros Town, with its abandoned docks. Most visitors come to Andros Town to stay at Small Hope Bay Lodge or to avail themselves of its facilities. The biggest retail industry, Androsia batik, is based in the area, too. The scuba diving minutes away on the barrier reef is what lures most visitors to this tiny place; others come here just for the shelling. On the opposite side of the water is Coakley Town. If you're driving, before you get to Andros Town, you may want to stop to spend some restful hours on the beach at Staniard Creek, another old settlement that feels like it drifted over from the South Seas.

Moving south from Andros Town, this part of Andros is the least developed and is studded with hundreds upon hundreds of palm trees. The Queen's Highway runs along the eastern coastline, but the only thing about this road that's regal is its name. In some 7km (4 1/3 miles), you can see practically the whole island. It's truly sleepy, and for that very reason, many people come here to get away from it all. You won't find much in the way of accommodations but you will find some places to crash (they're listed below).

The third and last major land area, South Andros, is the home of the wonderfully named Congo Town, where life proceeds at a snail's pace. The Queen's Highway, partially lined with pink-and-white conch shells, runs for about 40km (25 miles) or so. The island, as yet undiscovered, has some of the best beaches in The Bahamas, and you can enjoy them almost by yourself.

Another tiny island, undeveloped Mangrove Cay, is an escapist's dream, attracting naturalists and anglers, as well as a few divers. It's separated from Andros's northern and southern sections by bights (inland waterway). The settlements here got electricity and a paved road only in 1989. Mangrove Cay's best place for snorkeling and diving is Victoria Point Blue Hole (any local can point you there). Another village (don't blink as you pass through or you'll miss it) is Moxey Town, where you're likely to see fishermen unloading conch from fishing boats. Ferries, operated for free by the Bahamian government, ply back and forth over the waters separating Mangrove Cay from South Andros. At the end of the road in North Andros, private arrangements can be made to have a boat take you to Mangrove Cay.

Visitor Information

The Bahamas Ministry of Tourism maintains a branch office in Andros Town (tel. 242/368-2286). It's open Monday through Friday 9am to 5pm.

Fast Facts

ATMs Banks and ATMs are rare on Andros. There's one bank with an ATM on North Andros, Scotiabank, in Nicholl's Town (tel. 242/329-2700). The bank is open Monday through Thursday from 9:30am to 3pm, Friday from 9:30am to 4:30pm.

Emergencies To reach the police, call tel. 919 on North Andros, tel. 242/368-2626 on Central Andros, and tel. 242/369-4733 on South Andros.

Medical Care Government-run medical clinics are at Nicholl's Town on North Andros (tel. 242/329-2055), at Mangrove Cay on Central Andros (tel. 242/369-0089), and at Kemp's Bay on South Andros (tel. 242/369-4849).

Post Office The island's post office is in Nicholl's Town (tel. 242/329-2034), on North Andros. Hours are Monday through Friday from 9am to 4:30pm. Each little village on Andros has a store that serves as a post office, and hotel front desks can also sell Bahamian stamps. Make sure to mark cards and letters as airmail otherwise, you'll return home before they do.

Getting Around

Transportation can be a big problem on Andros. If you have to go somewhere, try to use one of the local taxis, though this can be a pricey undertaking.

The few rental cars available are in North and Central Andros. These are scarce, owing to the high costs of shipping cars here. The weather also takes a great toll on the cars that are brought in (salty air erodes metal), so no U.S. car-rental agencies are represented. Your best bet is to ask at your hotel to see what's available.

Anyway, it's not really recommended that you drive on Andros because roads are mainly unpaved and in bad condition, and gas stations are hard to find. Outlets for car rentals come and go faster than anybody can count. Renting a car is less formal, and less organized, than you might be used to.

The concierge at Andros's most upscale hotel, Kamaleme Cay, will arrange a cab or a rental car for you, but frankly, it's all word of mouth and terribly unlicensed and informal, with no options for purchase of additional insurance. Taxi drivers and owners of a handful of battered cars that can be rented will be at the airport in time for the landing of most major flights. You can negotiate a car rental on site or perhaps more safely and conveniently you can hire one of the local taxis to take you around. Rates run between $85 and $100 per day, plus gas. Be warned that sign postings and road conditions are horrible, but it's hard to get lost because the only road is the north-south, much-rutted thoroughfare known as Queen's Highway.

You may want to rent a bicycle, but you'll experience the same bad roads you would in a rental car. Guests of Small Hope Bay Lodge, Chickcharnie, and Mangrove Cay Inn can rent bikes at their hotels.

Accommodations

Accommodations on Andros

As the largest island of those inhabited in the Bahamas, there is a lot of space to cover; yet, Andros remains sparsely populated in comparison to other islands in the chain like Grand Bahama and New Providence. Still, Andros welcomes its fair share of tourists every year, each one with a different idea about how their trip is going to go. Fortunately the variation in types of available accommodations is suitable for pleasing a diverse crowd.

Hotels

You will find a few property types to consider in the area, including a bed & breakfast and a selection of hotels. Click on the links to read further info.

If you and your family would rather book your stay at a exclusive property, Kamalame Caywould be a nice place to start looking. With beautiful tropical furnishings, world-class amenities, stunning views, the rooms and suites at the Kamalame Cay offer everything people imagine a tropical paradise to be. The Marina and Beach Room have a fully stocked wet bar, Roman soaking tub, and a covered veranda. They're located on Staniard Creek.

Love At First Sight is a nice property on Andros. Set near Stafford Creek on North Andros is Love at First Sight, a fishing lodge with elegant accommodations that you might not expect from such a place. Guests will find them on Queen's Highway.

Another property worth considering will be Swains Cay Resort. Escape from the boring monotony of your everyday life with a trip to the tranquil Swains Cay Lodge. Guests will enjoy relaxing on the beach, or participating in the optional bone fishing tours that are available to guests of the resort. If you have questions, call them at (242) 369-0297.

Andros includes some other choices too. To read about other the standard hotels available, see "Hotel" page in this book.

Condos and Villa Complexes in Andros

If you are not in the market for a more typical hotel, you might think about renting one of the area's nearby condos or villas.

Knoll's Landing is one property found within Andros. Knoll's Landing is a family-friendly fishing lodge known for its laid-back atmosphere and great service. If you're looking to call before booking a room, you can do so at (242) 329-2039.

Some of the condo and villa complex possibilities are displayed in the chart below.

CONDO AND VILLA COMPLEXES IN ANDROS

Name	Type	Phone Number	Star Rating	Location	Island

Javarr's Twinberry Inn	Apartment building	(242) 369-5103		6.4 mi. East of Central South Andros Island	South Andros Island
Kroll's Landing	Villa complex	(242) 329-2039		27.0 mi. East of Central North Andros Island	North Andros Island

You can alternatively see all of the accommodations available for the Bahamas, when you visit Accommodation page of Bahamas website.

Camping and Eco-Tourism

Visitors who love the great outdoors might want to consider the selection of eco-tourist options offered on Andros.

Travelers hoping to stay on Andros will enjoy opportunities like Tiamo Resorts. Sitting on a private island in the outskirts of the Bahamas is this property, the ultimate in exclusive luxury hideaways. Guests will find the island and its surrounding waters alive with all things tropical, and free to enjoy and explore. Visitors will be able to find them at 1 Tiamo Beach Way, on Central Andros.

A destination on the oceanfront that merits consideration is Small Hope Bay Lodge. This all-inclusive lodge is a nature-lover's paradise. They offer a very relaxed setting that allows guests to do as much or as little as they like while they spend their days right on the beach. If you are looking to call before making reservations, you can do so at (242) 368-2014.

Those who love the outdoors will find a variety of different eco-lodges in the vicinity, including Mangrove Cay Club. Four bungalows on property house eight suits, built with high cypress ceilings and featuring large bedrooms, sitting rooms, bathrooms, and private porches with views of the ocean. The porches have rod rocks and buckets for soaking reels, as well as everything you need to take care of your equipment after a day of fishing. Reach them at (242) 369-0731.

Those planning to visit Andros will have many other eco-related accommodation choices too. You can read on Eco Tourism page regarding these types of properties if you'd like to learn some more information.

Individual Villas
Some favor the independence offered by one of the individual rental properties. Read on "Villa Rentals" page in this book for full information.

All-Inclusive Accommodations
Some travelers seek the added certainty of an all-inclusive package. There are several explanations why

this pricing method is popular. For instance, they provide a simple way to do everything you want without having to think about your budget.

Tiamo Resorts is one property southeastern Andros. Sitting on a private island in the outskirts of the Bahamas is this property, the ultimate in exclusive luxury hideaways. Guests will find the island and its surrounding waters alive with all things tropical, and free to enjoy and explore. They are located at 1 Tiamo Beach Way, on Central Andros.

One property on the waterfront worth mentioning is Small Hope Bay Lodge. This all-inclusive lodge is a nature-lover's paradise. They offer a very relaxed setting that allows guests to do as much or as little as they like while they spend their days right on the beach. For customers who want to call before you go, you can do so at (242) 368-2014.

All Inclusive

Andros All Inclusive Resorts

While you will certainly be able to stay at an all-inclusive hotel on Andros, it may not be the over-the-top experience people have come to expect when they hear the term. Rather than massive properties that serve as full and complete vacation destinations in their own right, here you'll find fishing lodges that with the inclusion of a room, food, and fishing excursions can be dubbed "all-inclusive." By offering food, several other small inns and guests houses have earned the title as well.

Some travelers love the convenience of an all-inclusive package. There are several explanations why these plans are so popular. Among other reasons, they let you go full blast without having to look different costs. Navigate the ones that interest you to find the most comprehensive details about food, amenities, activities, and more.

If you are trying to plan for some special occasion, or if you're traveling as a large party, think about a group-friendly property like Mangrove Cay Club. Four bungalows on property house eight suits, built with high cypress ceilings and featuring large bedrooms, sitting rooms, bathrooms, and private porches with views of the ocean. The porches have rod rocks and buckets for soaking reels, as well as everything you need to take care of your equipment after a day of fishing. If you have questions, call them at (242) 369-0731.

Deneki Outdoors Andros South is a property worth considering on Andros. Unpretentious for sure, Deneki Outdoors Andros South is a popular fishing lodge known for its staff that is knowledgeable in the area of local fishing. If you're looking for a bonefishing experience that you won't forget anytime soon, this is the spot for you. If you are looking to call before making reservations, you can do so at (242) 369-1408.

Bair's Lodge is another place to consider. Set in a plantation-style building with views of the ocean, each of the six bedrooms features terracotta floors, air conditioning, private bathrooms, and clean, comfortable linens. If you want to call ahead, you can do so at (242) 369-5060.

The table just below enables you to get some key facts concerning the 14 all-inclusive properties serving Andros.

ALL-INCLUSIVE ACCOMMODATIONS IN ANDROS					
Name	Type	Phone Number	Star Rating	Location	Island
Andros Bay Cottage	Lodge	(242) 368-5266		24.0 mi. North-Northwest of Central Congo Town	North Andros Island
Andros Beach Club	Hotel	(242) 369-		3.2 mi. North of Central	South Andros

Andros Island Travel and Tourism

		1454	South Andros Island	Island
Bair's Lodge	Lodge	(242) 369-5060	6.4 mi. East of Central South Andros Island	South Andros Island
Coral Caverns Dive Resort	Eco resort	(242) 368-5155	24.5 mi. North-Northwest of Central Congo Town	North Andros Island
Deneki Outdoors Andros South	Lodge	(242) 369-1408	1.1 mi. South of Central Congo Town	Central Andros
G J's Resort & Fishing Lodge	Lodge	(242) 329-2005	0.5 mi. Northeast of Central Nicholls Town	North Andros Island
Mangrove Cay Club	Lodge	(242) 369-0731	9.8 mi. Northwest of Central	Central Andros

				Congo Town	
Mars Bay Bonefish Lodge	Lodge	(242) 471-4296		9.5 mi. Southeast of Central South Andros Island	South Andros Island
Nathan's Lodge	Lodge	(242) 369-1707		9.9 mi. South of Central Congo Town	South Andros Island
Pleasant Bay Bonefish Lodge	Lodge	(242) 369-5551		7.8 mi. East-Southeast of Central South Andros Island	South Andros Island
Smal Hope Bay Lodge	Lodge	(242) 368-2014		2.2 mi. Northwest of Central Andros Town	Central Andros
Stafford Creek Lodge	Lodge	(242) 368-6050		15.1 mi. Northwest of Central Andros Town	North Andros Island
Tiamo	Eco	(242) 357-		2.7 mi. West-Northwest of	Central

Resorts	resort	2489	Central Congo Town	Andros
Tranquility Hill Bonefish Lodge	Lodge	(242) 368-4132	23.5 mi. North-Northwest of Central Congo Town	North Andros Island

Be aware of what exactly is covered in your all-inclusive plan as some places do not offer everything one might expect. Higher-end amenities such as spa services often incur an additional charge.

Eco Tourism

Eco Tourism Accommodations on Andros

In order to preserve the integrity of the land and optimize the already beautiful setting, many accommodations on Andros have become what they call "eco-friendly." Rather than bulldoze perfectly good land and create sprawling resorts, the buildings work in conjunction with what nature has already provided, and the owners and guests try to leave as little of a carbon footprint as possible. If this sounds like the type of place that you'd like to stay, you have certainly chosen the perfect destination.

Camping and Eco-Tourism in Andros
Nature enthusiasts and their families should consider the opportunities for eco-tourism in the area. Alongside the eco-lodges that are available, some unique eco-resorts are an alternative possibility. Click on the link to each accommodation to read additional info.

If you're trying to plan for a special occasion, or if you're traveling as a large group, you can find a group-friendly property like Mangrove Cay Club. Four bungalows on property house eight suits, built with high cypress ceilings and featuring large bedrooms, sitting rooms, bathrooms, and private porches with views of the ocean. The porches have rod rocks and buckets for soaking reels, as well as everything you need to take care of your equipment after a day of fishing. For customers who want to call ahead of time, do so at (242) 369-0731.

Deneki Outdoors Andros South is a property of this type, which is on Andros. Unpretentious for sure, Deneki Outdoors Andros South is a popular fishing lodge known for its staff that is knowledgeable in the area of local fishing. If you're looking for a bonefishing experience that you won't forget anytime soon, this is the spot for you. If you want to be sure they're open, call them at (242) 369-1408.

Those who love the outdoors will find a variety of different local eco-lodges. including Bair's Lodge. Set in a plantation-style building with views of the ocean, each of the six bedrooms features terracotta floors, air conditioning, private bathrooms, and clean, comfortable linens. If you are looking to call in advance, do so at (242) 369-5060.

The table right below summarizes more details regarding the 16 eco-tourism accommodations you can find.

ECO-ACCOMMODATIONS IN ANDROS					
Name	Type	Phone Number	Star Rating	Location	Island
Andros Bay Cottage	Lodge	(242) 368-5266		24.0 mi. North-Northwest of Central Congo Town	North Andros Island
Bair's Lodge	Lodge	(242) 369-5060		6.4 mi. East of Central South Andros Island	South Andros Island
Big Charlie's Lodge	Lodge	(242) 368-4297		22.8 mi. North-Northwest of	North Andros Island

Andros Island Travel and Tourism

Name	Type	Phone	Location	Area
			Central Congo Town	
Coral Caverns Dive Resort	Eco resort	(242) 368-5155	24.5 mi. North-Northwest of Central Congo Town	North Andros Island
Deneki Outdoors Andros South	Lodge	(242) 369-1408	1.1 mi. South of Central Congo Town	Central Andros
G J's Resort & Fishing Lodge	Lodge	(242) 329-2005	0.5 mi. Northeast of Central Nicholls Town	North Andros Island
Mangrove Cay Club	Lodge	(242) 369-0731	9.8 mi. Northwest of Central Congo Town	Central Andros
Mars Bay Bonefish Lodge	Lodge	(242) 471-4296	9.5 mi. Southeast of Central South	South Andros Island

				Andros Island	
Mount Pleasant Fishing Lodge	Lodge	(242) 368-5171		1.1 mi. South West of Central Andros Town	Central Andros
Nathan's Lodge	Lodge	(242) 369-1707		9.9 mi. South of Central Congo Town	South Andros Island
Pleasant Bay Bonefish Lodge	Lodge	(242) 369-5551		7.8 mi. East-Southeast of Central South Andros Island	South Andros Island
Small Hope Bay Lodge	Lodge	(242) 368-2014		2.2 mi. Northwest of Central Andros Town	Central Andros
Stafford Creek Lodge	Lodge	(242) 368-6050		15.1 mi. Northwest of Central Andros Town	North Andros Island
Tiamo	Eco	(242) 357-		2.7 mi. West-Northwest of	Central

Resorts	resort	2489	Central Congo Town	Andros
Tranquility Hill Bonefish Lodge	Lodge	(242) 368-4132	23.5 mi. North-Northwest of Central Congo Town	North Andros Island
Westside Fishing Resort	Eco resort	(242) 329-4026	0.2 mi. Northeast of Central Nicholls Town	North Andros Island

Fortunately, Andros has many other property types. if needing to find more details about other kinds of accommodations available for Andros should read on Accommodation page

Hotels

Hotels on Andros

The hotels available on Andros are as diverse as the people who visit the massive island. Whether you're the adventurous type who will be spending your days trekking about, or you're looking for a romantic retreat, there is a property that caters to your needs.

Hotels in Andros

There are multiple types of accommodations to select in the area, including a bed & breakfast and a selection of hotels. Click on their names to read additional details.

If you are trying to organize a conference or are traveling as a large party, consider a group-friendly accommodation such as Love At First Sight. Love At First Sight houses nine double rooms with twin double beds as well as one single room with one double bed for a total of 10 rooms. Each is vibrantly decorated, has a private bathroom, kitchenette, and WiFi. The property can be found on Queen's Highway.

One property positioned on the oceanfront you should consider is Swains Cay Resort. Escape from the boring monotony of your every day life with a trip to the tranquil Swains Cay Lodge. Guests will enjoy relaxing on the beach, or participating in the optional bonefishing tours that are available to guests of the resort. Visitors can reach them at (242) 369-0297.

Another good option available is Andros Island Bonefishing Club. Each room at the lodge features wonderful views of the ocean, which sits just steps from your front door. Keeping with the theme of modesty, the rooms are minimally decorated to give guests ample room for their fishing supplies. Call them at (242) 368-5167.

The chart right below lists more details on hotel possibilities.

HOTELS IN ANDROS

Name	Type	Phone Number	Star Rating	Location	Island
Andros Beach Club	Hotel	(242) 369-1454		3.2 mi. North of Central South Andros Island	South Andros Island
Andros Island Beach Resort	Cottages	(242) 329-1009		0.5 mi. Northeast of Central Nicholls Town	North Andros Island
Andros Island Bonefishing Club	Hotel	(242) 368-5167		24.5 mi. North-Northwest of Central Congo Town	North Andros Island
Conch Sound Resort Inn	Motel	(242) 329-2060		1.3 mi. Southeast of Central Nicholls	North Andros Island

Andros Island Travel and Tourism

Name	Type	Phone	Location	Area
			Town	
Kamalame Cay	Hotel	(876) 632-3213	25.2 mi. West-Southwest of Central Clifton Bay	North Andros Island
Love At First Sight	Hotel	(242) 368-6082	17.1 mi. South of Central Nicholls Town	North Andros Island
Mar & Mont Red Top Inn	Guest house	(242) 369-4612	Central Andros	North Andros Island
Pineville Motel	Motel	(242) 329-2788	0.3 mi. East-Northeast of Central Nicholls Town	North Andros Island
Quality Inn Staniard Creek	Hotel	(242) 368-6217	26.3 mi. South West of Central	North Andros Island

				Clifton Bay	
Seascape Inn	B & B	(242) 369-0342		8.2 mi. Northwest of Central Congo Town	Central Andros
Sunrise Inn on the Beach	Hotel	(242) 369-1640		17.8 mi. East-Southeast of Central North Andros Island	North Andros Island
Swains Cay Resort	Hotel	(242) 369-0297		7.2 mi. Northwest of Central Congo Town	Central Andros
Treasures of Andros	Cottages	(242) 359-1220		25.5 mi. South West of Central Clifton Bay	North Andros Island

Of course, Andros includes a full range of other types of properties. To reach our complete guide to other kinds of accommodations available for Andros, read on Accommodation page in this book.

Villa Rentals

Andros Rental Villas

Moreso than massive resort properties, what you'll encounter throughout Andros is a collection of privately owned villas and rental properties that guests are invited to make their own during their stay. Some are quaint and cabin like, while others are over-the-top and verging on mansions. The type of getaway you crave will help to determine which direction you choose to go with your rental.

Individual Villas

Anyone looking can find plenty of standalone villas on Andros. Many of them have a different style and type. The following table offers some key facts regarding the 16 available rental properties.

INDIVIDUAL VILLAS IN ANDROS

Name	Phone Number	Bedrooms	Bathrooms	Location	Island
Andros Beach House	(242) 369-1454	--	--	7.4 mi. Northeast of Central South Andros Island	South Andros Island
Coakley House	(786) 208-6540	4	4	0.5 mi. Northeast of Central Andros Town	North Andros Island
Coconut Beach	(407) 876-4025	3	2	1.2 mi. South-Southeast of Central Congo Town	Central Andros

Andros Island Travel and Tourism

Name	Phone	Bedrooms	Bathrooms	Location	Region
Coconut Palms Beach House	(800) 766-9137	--	--	9.3 mi. West of Central Congo Town	Central Andros
Ed and Emily Island Beach House Oasis	(242) 225-1988	2	1	8.0 mi. Northeast of Central South Andros Island	South Andros Island
Jeff's Beach House	(242) 369-5151	--	--	7.5 mi. Northwest of Central Congo Town	Central Andros
Monies on the Bay	(242) 441-4593	1	1	0.1 mi. North of Central Congo Town	Central Andros
Pleasant Dreams	(802) 349-6982	3	2	3.1 mi. Northwest of Central Nicholls Town	North Andros Island
Summer Wind	(305) 515-8785	2	1	2.1 mi. Southeast of Central Andros Town	North Andros Island

Sunset Point	(242) 368-2033	3	3	1.0 mi. West-Southwest of Central Andros Town	North Andros Island
The Beach House	(416) 709-7441	2	--	0.5 mi. East-Northeast of Central Nicholls Town	North Andros Island
The Retreat at Pleasant Harbor	(802) 388-7507	3	1	0.8 mi. North of Central Nicholls Town	North Andros Island
VRBO Listing #3004261ha	(242) 336-3548	2	2	0.7 mi. North of Central Andros Town	North Andros Island
VRBO Listing #332915ha	(800) 766-9137	2	2	1.3 mi. South-Southeast of Central Congo Town	Central Andros
VRBO Listing #335647ha	(242) 455-6943	--	--	0.3 mi. Northeast of Central	North Andros Island

				Andros Town	
VRBO Listing #346557ha	(954) 681-4818	3	2	7.5 mi. Northeast of Central South Andros Island	South Andros Island

If you are seeking more accommodations beyond this category, you should consider other locations. To learn more about other kinds of accommodations for Andros, read on Accommodation page in this book.

Transportation

Where you'll stay on Andros could determine your mode of transportation

Measuring in at 2,300 square miles, Andros is the largest island in the Bahamas – yet it remains largely undeveloped. This makes it a haven for tourists interested in experiencing the natural side of the islands and who want to take advantage of Mother Nature's bounty. Before tourists can get their kicks visiting the famed Blue Holes, diving around the third largest barrier reef in the world, or taking a hike to do some bird watching, they have to work out how they'll get to the island, and then, how they'll get around when they arrive.

Getting There

When it comes to traveling to Andros Island, you have two options: fly or sail. If you're flying, there are four airports serviced by both commercial and charter airlines, while those who are sailing will have to determine whether they'll captain their own boat or hire a crew.

Getting Around

Although technically considered to be one island, Andros actually consists of three major islands known as North Andros, Mangrove Cay, and South Andros, as well as a collection of small islets. These islands are not connected by land bridges, so although rental cars and taxis are a major source of transportation, tourists who want to see as much of Andros as possible will likely have to spend some time sailing.

Air Travel

Despite the small number of tourists who visit Andros on a regular basis, flying to this island is no more difficult than many other more popular spots in the Bahamas. There are four airports on the island, all of which are located along the east coast spare one, but spread out enough so that you'll be able to fly as near your accommodations as possible without having to spend hours driving to get to your final destination. These airports, listed by location from north to south, are San Andros Airport (SAQ), Andros Town International Airport (ASD), Congo Town Airport (COX), and the Clarence A. Bain Airport (MAY). San Andros Airport and Andros Town International Airport have regularly scheduled flights from New Providence Island and Ft. Lauderdale in the United States, and all three welcome chartered flights as needed.

Sailing

You can't plan a getaway on Andros without considering sailing as an important source of transportation. Because this group is so close to the coast of the U.S. state of Florida, it is a very popular sailing destination. There are a few things those who have plans to sail themselves should be aware of, such as the fact that the calm waters on the west coast can be deceiving, and that there are a staggering four different ports of entry on the island. You can learn everything you need to know about what it takes to sail to Andros, as well as get a few tips on participating in sailing excursions hosted by locals when you read Sailing & Boating page in this book.

Rental Cars

On the mainland of Andros there are 65 miles of roadways that stretch from Morgan's Bluff to Behring Point. Tourists who are aged 21 and up can rent a vehicle from the airport or in any of the major settlements for between $70 and $120(USD) a day as long as they have a valid driver's license from home. Rental agencies here are locally owned, and your rental agreement will likely be so informal that there will be no paperwork involved, and some spots only accept cash.

The chart on Car Rentals page has contact information for rental agencies on Andros, allowing you to call ahead and find out specific policies.

The roads on the island are rather poorly developed, so proceed with caution wherever you drive, and remember to keep to the left side of the road when you're behind the wheel.

Taxis

Independent taxi operators pick up the slack for tourists who decide not to rent a car when vacationing on Andros. You'll find them camped out at the airports when known flights land, and also by the ferry docks to pick up those who arrive by sea. If you're looking for a ride elsewhere on the island, you'll likely have to call to have someone pick you up.

Rates are set by the government, based upon a two person occupancy. Passengers pay $3 to ride, plus an additional $0.40(USD) per quarter mile. Extra passengers are $3(USD) a piece, and if you have more than two pieces of luggage per person, you'll pay extra for those as well. If your driver gave you good service, 15 percent tip is the norm.

Ferries

As you might imagine, ferries play an important role in travel around Andros, as well as the rest of the Bahamas. If you're hoping to visit several different islands, you can utilize one of two different ferry operations that service the island. One is the slow-moving government run Mail Boat which is typically chosen by those traveling on a budget, and the other is Bahamas Ferries, which are much faster but also more expensive.

For more detailed information about ferry service to Andros, read Ferries page in this book.

A trip to Andros involves a lot of planning, and you should begin with choosing your transportation. Take into account where you'll stay, travel time, and cost as you begin to make your decisions and you'll find yourself easily led in one direction over another.

Air Travel

Andros Air Travel
Expect some limitations when flying into any of the Andros Islands

Regardless of which airport you choose to fly into, your first order of business will be to make a connecting flight at the Lynden Pindling International Airport on New Providence Island. It takes around 15 minutes from New Providence Island.

Andros, which is actually a series of three main islands and a few islets and cays, is 2,300 square miles in area, so it makes sense that there would be four different airports serving the island. Strategically placed, mostly along the east coast, these airports are small facilities with minimal extras. Unfortunately, two of them only accept charter planes.

Flying Domestic

Other than short hops from Lynden Pindling International Airport, no direct flights regularly come into Andros Island. Even then, only Western Air provides regular service – to two of the four airports. This means you should book early and, if you must fly, plan your vacation for areas around the two airports: Congo Town Airport and San Andros Airport. The other two airports on the island only receive charter planes, which is an option for anyone already in the Caribbean or South Florida. Still for most people, Congo Town and San Andros Airports are the only options.

CLARENCE A. BAIN AIRPORT CARIBBEAN FLIGHTS

To/From	Airport Code	Airlines
New Providence Island, Bahamas	NAS	Flamingo Air, Performance Air

CONGO TOWN AIRPORT CARIBBEAN FLIGHTS

To/From	Airport Code	Airlines
New Providence Island, Bahamas	NAS	Performance Air, Western Air

SAN ANDROS AIRPORT CARIBBEAN FLIGHTS

To/From	Airport Code	Airlines

Freeport, Grand Bahama Island	FPO	Regional Air
New Providence Island, Bahamas	NAS	Western Air

Once you land, it is suggested that you make ground transportation arrangements right at the airport. Taxi and rental car services are limited on the island, and it is best to set things up where they are most likely to be.

With multiple airports through Andros, tourists have options when it comes to flying to the island. Make sure to review the location of the airport with regards to where you'll be staying or where the bulk of the activities you'll be participating in are located to prevent even more unplanned for travel time and you should have no trouble when you choose to fly to your Andros vacation.

You can take a look at this chart to help you call one of the regional air charter services.

CHARTER OPERATORS

Name	Phone	Location	Island
Flamingo Air at MAY	(242) 351-4963	Clarence A. Bain Airport - Central Andros	Central Andros
LeAir Andros Office	(242) 368-2919	Andros Town International Airport - 1.7 mi. (2.7 km) South of Andros Town	North Andros Island
LeAir Mangrove Cay	(242) 369-0020	Clarence A. Bain Airport - Central Andros	Central Andros
Regional Air Charter at SAQ	(242) 329-7108	San Andros Airport - 27.9 mi. (44.9 km) Northwest of Andros Town	North Andros Island

Ferries

Ferries to Andros

Ferries are perhaps the most important form of transportation for Andros

For years the only way to get from place to place in the Bahamas was by boat. Now, you'll find an air strip at the very least on many of the most visited islands, but still, ferry services make the rounds. Andros is one of the islands in the chain that benefits from these ferries, and tourists can opt to take to the seas rather than the skies.

Riding the Ferries

Andros is serviced by two major ferries. The first is the government run Mail Boats that were originally brought into being as a way to deliver mail and freight to the Out Islands. Now, passengers can ride as well, though the boats continue chugging along at a slow pace. In trade for a long trip, you'll spend less money than flying or using the faster service available. The boats fail from Potter's Cay on New Providence Island, and take about six hours to make the journey. You can find schedules and fares by contacting the Dock Master on the phone at 242-393-1064.

Bahamas Ferries is the other, faster option available. There are two boats owned by the company called Sea Link and Sea Wind, which also originate in Nassau, yet only take two hours to get to Fresh Creek and two and a half hours to get to Driggs Hill.

Familiarize yourself with the choices for water transportation below.

FERRY DOCKS

Name	Location
Fresh Creek Ferry Terminal	1.8 mi. (2.9 km) Southeast of Andros Town
Morgan's Bluff Harbor Dock	34.5 mi. (55.6 km) North-Northwest of Andros Town

Whether you're willing to pay for speed or enjoy the leisurely pace of a Mail Boat, travel by ferry is certainly available to those who need it to get to their getaway on Andros.

FERRY ROUTES, ANDROS				
Location Served	Dock A	Dock B	Company	Frequency
Nassau	Fresh Creek Ferry Terminal	Bahamas Ferries Potters Cay Dock	Bahamas Ferries	1 to 2 days per week

Rental Cars

Car Rentals on Andros
Rental cars help tourists cover a lot of ground on Andros

There is a lot of land to cover on Andros. At 2,300 square miles, it is the largest island in the Bahamas, and the fifth largest overall in the Caribbean. Much of this space remains undeveloped, which means in many areas public transportation is lacking. For this reason, renting a car is the recommended course of action for those who will be doing a lot of exploring.

Renting a Car

From coast to coast, there are numerous places to rent a car on Andros, all of which are locally owned and operated. In many cases, this means you'll encounter an informal rental agreement that involves the shake of a hand rather than a signed document. If this makes you uncomfortable, simply ask for something in writing. You'll need to be over the age of 21 to rent at each location, as well as be in possession of a valid driver's license from your country of origin. Since every location is different, make sure to call ahead and ask if there are any specific regulations you need to be aware of.

Michael Thomson

Take a look at the following chart for the rental agencies serving Andros.

VEHICLE RENTAL COMPANIES			
Name	Phone	Location	Island
Adderley's Car Rental	(242) 357-2149	3.4 mi. (5.5 km) Northwest of Andros Town	North Andros Island
Bill Arguiles Rentals	(242) 357-2149	1.0 mi. (1.6 km) Northwest of Andros Town	North Andros Island
Brian Moxey's Car Rental	(242) 369-0353	Central Andros	Central Andros
Cargill's Rental Car	(242) 368-2658	0.7 mi. (1.1 km) North-Northwest of Andros Town	North Andros Island
D&E Rent-A-Car	(242) 368-2454	3.9 mi. (6.3 km) Northwest of Andros Town	North Andros Island
Executive Car	(242)	0.9 mi. (1.4 km)	North

Andros Island Travel and Tourism

Rentals	329-2081	Northwest of Andros Town	Andros Island
GJ's Car Rental	(242) 329-2005	Queen's Highway - Nicholls Town	North Andros Island
Green's Car Rental	(242) 369-3593	South Andros Island	South Andros Island
King's Supply	(242) 369-0478	Central Andros	Central Andros
Lenglo Rental Car	(242) 369-1702	South Andros Island	South Andros Island
Mal-Jack's Rental	(242) 369-3679	South Andros Island	South Andros Island
R&S Enterprise	(242) 329-3305	26.3 mi. (42.3 km) North-Northwest of Andros Town	North Andros Island
Rahming's	(242)	South Andros Island	South

Rental	369-1608		Andros Island
Rooney's Auto	(242) 368-2255	Andros Town	North Andros Island
Shorrs Car Rentals	(242) 368-6140	15.6 mi. (25.1 km) Northwest of Andros Town	North Andros Island
Thompson Brothers Rental	(242) 368-2166	16.5 mi. (26.6 km) South of Andros Town	North Andros Island
Tropical Car Rentals	(242) 329-2515	Nicholls Town	North Andros Island

Driving on Andros

From Morgan's Bluff to Behring Point, you'll have the opportunity to drive on 65 miles of roads on Andros. The roads here are rugged, which is part of the island's natural charm, but it doesn't make it easy for them to drive on. Visitors are instructed to proceed with caution, driving slow and paying close attention to the road so you are not caught off guard by pot holes. Also, remember to keep to the left side of the road, which is how traffic moves on the island.

Rental Costs

The cost of your rental will vary depending on who you rent with and what type of vehicle you request. In general, the range is from $70 to $120(USD), not including the cost of insurance. Be aware that some locations only accept cash, so make sure you have enough on hand.

Gas Stations

If you've got plans to go-go-go during your stay on Andros, it is in your best interest to consider renting a car. There are a few things to be aware of like the fact that many locations don't accept credit cards, but these are kinks that can be worked out with a simple phone call to the agency of your choice.

Sailing & Boating

Sailing and Boating Near Andros
Sail into the horizon and back again by planning some time in the seas that surround Andros Islands

Not all of Andros is able to be seen on wheels, so when roadways run out, locals and tourists must rely on boats to get by. Many of the large resorts offer sailing trips as part of their packages, but you can also hire a private charter, or rent a boat to sail yourself. Sailors should steer clear of the west coast where shoals make conditions dangerous, but the east coast offers smooth sailing.

In keeping with the island's eco- and adventure-tourism themes, sailing is a popular way to get to Andros. There are two full-service marinas, one in Fresh Creek and the other in Stanyard Creek, on the island in addition to several other docking facilities around the perimeter of the island.

Docking

Before you can officially begin your vacation on this island, you'll have to clear customs. To do so, you'll approach Andros with your yellow quarantine flag flying and place a call over your VHF radio on channel 16 to let officials know you are on your way. You'll be directed to one of the island's official ports of entry, either in Fresh Creek, Mangrove Cay, Morgan's Bluff, or San Andros, where an official will meet you. At this point only the captain may leave the vessel as the official reviews all of the appropriate paperwork and issues immigration forms to everyone on board. Once cleared, you'll be charged somewhere between $150 and $300(USD) depending on the length of your boat. This fee covers not only your cruising permit, but also a fishing permit and the prepayment of your departure fee. When this has been paid, you are free to head to the marina of your choice, and you're legally allowed to continue to sail in the area of up to 90 days.

Planning to reach Andros using your own vessel, or one you charter? Check out the table that follows to find basic information for area marinas.

MARINAS

Name	Phone	Location
Kamalame Cay Marina	(242) 368-6281	10.6 mi. (17.1 km) Northwest of Andros Town
Lighthouse Yacht Club and Marina	(242) 368-2305	Andros Town
Morgan's Bluff Commercial Dock	--	34.5 mi. (55.6 km) North-Northwest of Andros Town

A day of sailing around the Andros Islands can be unpredicable, and bring a lot of joy. Whether you sail directly to the islands as your main form of international travel or charter a yacht for a day of island hopping, spending time out at sea is a great way to spend part of your vacation.

Taxis

Andros Taxis
Calling for a cab is never a problem on Andros
Although it is recommended for tourists staying on Andros to rent a car in order to see as much of the island as possible, this option is not for everyone. Fortunately, taxis are available in abundance, ready to get tourists who don't want to drive themselves where they need and want to go.

Taxi Companies

You'll find taxis waiting to pick up passengers at the airports and ferry terminals, and on occasion you'll spot one on the streets and be able to wave the driver down. Still, your best option for ensuring you have a ride is to call any one of the many local taxi operators and have a driver pick you up.

Check out the chart that follows for contact information for local taxis.

TAXI SERVICES			
Name	Phone	Location	Island
Allen Russell Taxi Service	(242) 357-2876	Lowe Sound - North Andros Island	North Andros Island
Carlos Saunders Taxi Service	(242) 239-4224	Mastic Point - North Andros Island	North Andros Island
Cecil Gaitor Taxi Service	(242) 357-2705	Mastic Point - North Andros Island	North Andros Island
Henson Saunders Taxi Service	(242) 464-3151	Mastic Point - North Andros Island	North Andros Island
John Saunders Taxi Service	(242) 329-7137	Fire Road - North Andros Island	North Andros Island
Lee Meadows Taxi	(242)	Mars Bay - South	South

Andros Island Travel and Tourism

Name	Phone	Location	Area
Service	369-5029	Andros Island	Andros Island
Linden Farrington Taxi Service	(242) 464-3029	Cargill Creek - Central Andros	Central Andros
Peter Russel Taxi Service	(242) 329-4224	San Andros - North Andros Island	North Andros Island
Renford Argo Taxi Service	(242) 368-2030	Andros Hope - Central Andros	Central Andros
Reverend Newton Hamilton Taxi Service	(242) 471-4722	Fresh Creek - Central Andros	Central Andros
Rowena Sands Taxi Service	(242) 369-5028	Pleasant Bay - South Andros Island	South Andros Island
Rupert Pinder Taxi Service	(242) 368-2030	Love Hill - Central Andros	Central Andros
Sabrina Johnson Taxi Service	(242) 368-2579	Love Hill - Central Andros	Central Andros
Shirley Forbes Taxi Service	(242) 369-2930	Congo Town Airport - Congo	Central Andros

		Town	
Wilfred Sherman Taxi Service	(242) 368-2030	Stafford Creek - Central Andros	Central Andros
William Adderley Taxi Service	(242) 357-2149	Fresh Creek - Central Andros	Central Andros

Rates, Fares, and Fees

What you need to know about the cost of taking a taxi on Andros is that the rates have been preset by the government so you'll not be able to negotiate for a lower fare. Passengers pay $3(USD) to get into the cab, then $0.40(USD) for every quarter mile traveled. These rates are based on two passenger occupancy, and you'll pay an extra $3(USD) per person if more people are traveling with you. You may store two pieces of luggage in the trunk for free, but anything beyond that will cost extra.

Often, people who get along with their drivers will hire them to pick them up later on and take them on a tour of a particular area. These prices should be discussed with your driver, as these prices can be decided outside of the set rates. Whether you take a quick ride or do hire your driver for a tour, make sure to set aside an extra 15 percent or more for a tip.

Friendly drivers and reasonable prices make taxis a great option for local transportation when you're staying on Andros. Keep this in mind as an alternative option, even if you do decide to rent a car

Restaurants

Andros Restaurants

While there are a few known restaurants on Andros, dining here will be a surprise for many. Food is often prepared in the kitchen of the inn you're staying with, at a pop-up barbecue joint alongside the beach, and of course there are few restaurants in the style that most people are familiar with. Be prepared to dine on a lot of seafood since it is easy to come by and always fresh.

Caribbean and Local

Unfortunately, vacationers will only have one chance to enjoy local dishes on Andros. Find out more about it below.

The Great House is located at Kamalame Cay and is a bar and grill located within Andros. Honoring the elaborate great houses of the plantation era in the Bahamas, the Great House at Kamalame Cay mixes the casual atmosphere of island life with just a dash of elegance in its decor. They're located on Staniard Creek.

CARIBBEAN AND LOCAL RESTAURANTS ON ANDROS

Name	Location	Island	Type	Phone Number
The Great	10.7 mi. Northwest of Central Andros	North Andros	Caribbean	(876) 632-3213

House   Town   Island

Weather

Weather in the Bahamas

The weather of the Bahamas offers travelers warm sun and cooling winds

The weather in the Bahamas is a treat for travelers. Although the chain is made up of over 700 low-lying islands stretching from just east of Florida down into the Caribbean, most of the islands have very similar climates.

The Bahamas temperatures are moderated by the warm waters of the Gulf Stream. Additionally, because the Bahamas are closer to continental North America - and thus more easily effected by North American cold air systems - they are slightly cooler than other Caribbean islands.

Average temperatures in the Bahamas range from 80 to 90 degrees Fahrenheit (27 to 32 degrees Celsius) in the summer to 70 to 80 degrees Fahrenheit (21 to 27 degrees Celsius) in the winter. The northern Bahamian islands can be even a little cooler. Winds across the Bahamas keep vacations cool in the daytime and help lower the temperatures at night. Relative humidity is about 65% throughout the year, making temperatures feel a little warmer than they read at times.

The islands rainy season lasts from May to October, dropping an average of 4.3 inches of rain each month. October sees the heaviest amount, with approximately 8.10 inches, and June comes in at a close second with an average of 8.9 inches of rain. Still the Bahamas experiences about 310 days of sunshine each year, and averages 8 hours per day.

Although the Bahamas is located in the hurricane belt that lies across most of the Caribbean, many storms bypass the island chain and instead circle below it before heading north toward the United States. Of course, the islands are equipped to respond to a storm if one does hit.

Modern technology offers some reassurance to travelers who want to visit the Caribbean during the hurricane season, which lasts from June to November. Because hurricanes can be tracked from the time they form, travelers should have no problem preparing and canceling travel plans if necessary.

The table below contains selected climatological data for the Bahamas as reported at Nassau International Airport. While some islands are dryer than others, the climate throughout the Bahamas is fairly uniform; this table should give you a good idea of what the weather will be like in a given month, and what trends to expect during your vacation.

Michael Thomson

Month	Average Daily High Temperature	Average Daily Low Temperature	Average Monthly Precipitation	% Days with Rain
January	77.00°F	64.30°F	1.59 in	24.8%
February	77.10°F	64.70°F	1.61 in	26.2%
March	79.00°F	66.30°F	1.55 in	23.2%
April	80.90°F	68.50°F	2.26 in	19.7%
May	84.00°F	72.20°F	4.97 in	32.5%
June	87.10°F	75.60°F	7.01 in	43.2%
July	89.00°F	77.00°F	6.00 in	44.8%
August	89.20°F	77.10°F	6.46 in	50.3%
September	88.30°F	76.20°F	7.21 in	55.1%
October	85.20°F	74.00°F	6.56 in	35.6%
November	81.90°F	70.90°F	2.63 in	25.8%
December	78.30°F	66.40°F	1.59 in	24.1%

All in all, the weather in the Bahamas offers travelers cooling winds and warm temperatures to enjoy nearly every day of their journey.

Michael Thomson

www.ingramcontent.com/pod-product-compliance
Lightning Source LLC
Chambersburg PA
CBHW021105080526
44587CB00010B/390